Forgive,
Let Go, and
Live

Forgive, Let Go, and Live

DEBORAH SMITH PEGUES

HARVEST HOUSE PUBLISHERS
EUGENE, OREGON

All the incidents described in this book are true. The author has changed people's names to protect their privacy except for the facts already published in a contributor's own works or in news accounts.

Cover by Franke Design and Illustration, Excelsior, Minnesota

Cover illustration © cundra / iStock

FORGIVE, LET GO, AND LIVE
Copyright © 2015 by Deborah Smith Pegues
Published by Harvest House Publishers
Eugene, Oregon 97402
www.harvesthousepublishers.com

Library of Congress Cataloging-in-Publication Data
Pegues, Deborah Smith, 1950-
Forgive, let go, and live / Deborah Smith Pegues.
    pages cm
ISBN 978-0-7369-6222-3 (pbk.)
ISBN 978-0-7369-6223-0 (eBook)
1. Forgiveness—Religious aspects—Christianity. 2. Forgiveness. I. Title.
BV4647.F55P44 2015
234'.5—dc23
                                        2014048810

Printed in the United States of America

15 16 17 18 19 20 21 22 23 / BP-JH / 10 9 8 7 6 5 4 3 2 1

This book is dedicated to my late spiritual mentor,
Dr. Juanita Smith,
who taught and modeled true forgiveness.

Acknowledgments

People often say TEAM is an acronym for Together Everyone Accomplishes More; they are right. I could not have completed this project without the team of prayer intercessors and the anonymous and named people who told their stories. Special thanks to:

Pastor Edward and Vanessa Smith of the Zoe Christian Fellowship (ZCF) of Whittier, California, for their leadership and motivation to walk by faith in every endeavor.

My prayer team included: Jeanette Stone and my ZCF Life Group; Sandy Grubb, fellow member of the World Vision USA board of directors who reminded the board *daily* to pray for the completion of the manuscript; Suellen Roberts and members of the Christian Women in Media Association president's club, Raynae Hernandez, Sylvia Gardner, Yvonne Gibson Johnson, Billie Rodgers, Diane Gardner, Judge Mablean Ephraim, Marva Sykes, Verna Pierce, Cathy and Ralph Lawson, Diane Kelly, Darrell and Maisha Henry, and my social media community who constantly offered daily prayers and words of encouragement.

My long-time friends, Alvin and Pamela Kelley, and Kelvin and Delisa Kelley kept me balanced through the entire writing process by generously sharing their vacation facilities, planning short getaways, and being my ever-willing informal survey group when I needed immediate feedback on my ideas, assumptions, and conclusions. My "input team," informal editors, and reviewers deserve special recognition: Sheronne Burke, LaVerne Allen, Sylvia Malzman, Ennis Smith,

Karen Mace, Jennifer Hamner, T. Faye Griffin, Tammy V., Jeanetta Douglas, Alexus Davis, Marva Morrison, and Maisha Henry.

Of course, without the personal stories and contributions, there would be no book. I'm thankful for the brave and obedient men and women who have experienced freedom in forgiving and cared enough to share their victories with the world.

I offer high praise to my Harvest House publishing team. Bob Hawkins (president), Terry Glaspey (acquisitions director), Rod Morris (editor extraordinaire), and the entire staff give new meaning to the power of teamwork—all for the glory of God.

Finally, I'm eternally grateful to God for my husband, Darnell Pegues. From encouragement to technical support to research to manuscript proofing, he's a precious asset that I treasure deeply. Thank you, Sweetheart, for loving God and for loving me.

Contents

PART 3: Decisions, Decisions: The Forgiveness Process

PART 4: Forgiveness Is Good for You: Exploring the Benefits and Rewards

Forgiveness Prayers for Life's Hurts and Injustices

Prologue

Why Forgiving Is So Hard

"Even as a little girl, when kids would cross me in any way, I never let them back into my good graces."

My mom's words echoed in my spirit and found rest there for many years of my life. Similarly, my father never forgot a single offense that anybody committed against him. He and my mom argued frequently about things that happened or had been said in the far distant past. They served faithfully and sacrificially inside and outside the walls of the church. Nevertheless, a spirit of unforgiveness plagued them.

Just days before my dad passed away at age 78, I had the privilege of reconciling him and his best friend after a three-year rift. They were fellow members of their church trustee board and had disagreed over a financial transaction. Prior to their split, they had enjoyed rich fellowship and great family fun over their 50-year history. Notwithstanding, Dad believed the church had treated him unfairly (I didn't agree with him based on the facts *he* presented) and he was not going to let it go—especially in light of his extreme generosity and long-term service. Through much prayer and long conversations in which I reminded him of the consequences of unforgiveness, he finally relented—or, I should say, *repented*.

My mom, who passed away four years later at 82, frequently recounted the many instances of my dad's physical and verbal abuse. After 21 years of marriage, she'd finally mustered the courage to literally escape to another state with five dependent boys in tow (my older brother and I had already left the nest). They remained separated for 40 years but never divorced. I'm convinced it was bitterness that ushered her into her 10-year battle with dementia prior to her death. All of her imaginary conversations had an angry tone and centered on her painful issues with my dad.

My parents' legacy of holding on to offenses influenced how we, their seven children, dealt with people who offended or crossed us. With such a heritage, I knew unforgiveness was poised to become a stronghold in my life. The pattern had already started to evolve. If people offended me, I never viewed them the same. Depending on the nature of the relationship, I would either keep my emotional distance or make a mental note never to trust, favor, or include them again in my dealings. My most common tactic was to hide behind being "too busy" to interact with them again—ever. They finally got the message: Once you offend Deborah, you are out. No three strikes policy here!

Shortly after I married my wonderful husband, I sternly warned him, "Please try not to do anything where I'll have to forgive you because unforgiveness runs in my family. We do absolutely no forgiving!" This statement seems hilarious to me today, but I was dead serious at the time I said it.

It was not until I met one of my most beloved spiritual mentors, the late Dr. Juanita Smith, that I began to make headway in conquering this emotional giant. She taught and modeled forgiveness on a level I'd never seen. She frequently proclaimed, "I release everybody who has hurt me." She didn't just give lip service to the idea; I watched her walk it out many times.

I finally decided that unforgiveness had wreaked havoc in my life long enough. It had caused me to write off several relatives, friends, coworkers, and others. I spent way too much time in my head rehearsing the wrongs people perpetrated against me and imagining the awful things I could have said or done to retaliate if I weren't a Christian. I started to realize how counterproductive it is to engage in such thinking. So, as an act of faith and obedience to God, I declared my freedom from unforgiveness. It was and is a giant I could never conquer in my own strength.

You may be asking, "Why is forgiving others such a hard thing for so many to do—even strong Christians?" I believe when we have been damaged, deprived, or disadvantaged by another, we instinctively want to be compensated for our loss. The loss can take any number of forms, including property, affection, freedom, self-esteem, innocence, and physical well-being.

Every offense is an assault on our emotions. The root meaning of *emotion* is "to move." When our emotions are attacked, we want to move against the offender. But when the law or our better judgment or other circumstances prevent us from moving to exact revenge, to gain justice, or to be made whole, anger rears its head. Some people choose to bury their anger. In doing so, they develop a root of bitterness that can quickly infiltrate their hearts and minds—stealing their joy and turning them into someone they don't want to be.

This book will show you a better way to handle the inevitable offenses of life. I hope that as you read the following pages, you'll look at how you deal with your hurts and make a commitment to walk in forgiveness—no matter what!

In Part 1, we will take a brief walk down Revenge Row and

see how retaliation impacted the lives of those who refused to forgive, let go, and move forward.

In Part 2, a number of contributors share their heart-wrenching, as well as heartwarming, stories of deciding to release the perpetrator of their hurtful experiences. I have changed the names and circumstances to protect their privacy except where the facts are disclosed in their published writings or in news reports. I make no attempt to weigh the magnitude of the offenses as they are each so personal. From being a victim of gossip to enduring the horror of rape to financial rip-offs, these forgivers will inspire, challenge, and motivate you to let it go.

In Part 3, faith and practicality converge as we explore and debunk the myths of what forgiveness is and what it is not. I hope the guidelines I present for working through the forgiving process will transform your thinking and move you to a higher quality of life.

In Part 4, we'll look at the spiritual, emotional, relational, physical, and yes, even financial benefits of forgiveness. The Holy Spirit's illumination of these truths will challenge you to grow and to go forward as a model and ambassador of forgiveness in a revengeful world.

Finally, the "Forgiveness Prayers" at the back of the book address a variety of hurts and offenses and will guide you in praying to release the person who has harmed you and to stand in faith for your deliverance from unforgiveness. Through these Scripture-based, courageous prayers and faith declarations, God will surely turn your ashes into beauty.

Part 1

An Eye for an Eye
Stories from Revenge Row

1

Christopher Dorner
Police Officer Turns Menace to Society

"Those who use the sword will die by the sword."

MATTHEW 26:52 NLT

"Deborah, have you been watching the news about that fired police officer who's out to get revenge?" It was my friend George. I had anticipated his call.

A few years ago I had counseled him through his extreme anger and frustration with the police department of a major US city. His dream of joining the police force had gone up in smoke during his training at the police academy. He had made the courageous but politically unwise decision to denounce police brutality against a recent victim. Shortly thereafter, he was kicked out of the academy on a flimsy excuse and flatly told off the record that he would *never* be hired to work for the police department in that city.

He was devastated. I had prayed earnestly with and for him that God would touch his heart and cause him not to seek revenge. The prayers worked. By the grace of God, I was able to convince him that the police department's rejection was God's protection. Who knows what negative detour his life would have taken had he made the police force?

Now, as I listened to his highly animated voice, I became

16

concerned that the Christopher Dorner situation would reopen old wounds.

"You know I was there mentally at one point," George continued. "That could be me hunkered down in that cabin. But I thought about my mom, my children, and the rest of my family. I knew it would really hurt everybody if I'd done something like that. Dorner has a legitimate beef though, Deborah. Somebody has to bring the police department's problems to light. If this is what it takes, so be it."

I winced at the thought that my friend, like numerous others in the minority community who had weighed in on the drama that unfolded over the past 48 hours, might be condoning Dorner's actions. I reminded him that nothing could justify the killings.

When our conversation ended, I went online to research more facts about the case and to read Dorner's 11,000-word "manifesto" that he'd sent to various news organizations explaining his behavior. Here's a quick review of the circumstances that led to the events that had the entire city on edge.

In July 2007, Officer Christopher Dorner and his partner were called to a public disturbance where a disorderly, mentally challenged man was creating a nuisance. Dorner later reported to department officials that his partner had used excessive force during the arrest, kicking the man in the face while he was handcuffed. The department investigated the incident and decided that Dorner's claim was not true. They fired him in 2008 for making a false report.

He charged racism and appealed his case for job reinstatement. He exhausted every level of the police department's appeals process to no avail. He went on to file a wrongful termination lawsuit through local and state courts; they upheld the department's decision.

In February 2013, consumed with rage, Dorner decided his only option was to retaliate. He went on a shooting spree from February 2 through February 12 against specific officers and their families. He killed four people, including three police officers, and wounded four other officers. He became the subject of the largest manhunt in the history of that city's police. Acting on a tip, the police finally tracked him to a cabin in the mountains. He died there on February 12, 2013, from a self-inflicted gunshot wound to the head during a standoff with the police. He was 33 years old.

In reading Dorner's manifesto,[1] I observed five toxic, erroneous, and overall "bad beliefs" that ultimately derailed his destiny and caused untold heartache for his family and the families of his victims. The truth is that any of us could fall prey to these beliefs.

Bad Belief 1: The Bible is not a guidebook for everyday living. Referring to it as "that old book, made of fiction and limited non-fiction," Dorner pooh-poohed the idea of turning the other cheek—going as far to say that "Jesus was never called a nigger." No, He wasn't, but He was ridiculed, beaten, and crucified. Plus, He knew that only God has the right to avenge wrongs.

Bad Belief 2: The value of a person's life is measured by career success. Many people, especially men, define their worth by their work. Unfortunately, when an economic downturn, a firing, or other adverse circumstance brings their employment or ability to make money to a screeching halt, they feel worthless and powerless. This response is a result of a bad belief system. Oh, that Dorner would have known and embraced the truth that we are all created with an intrinsic value and have a Divine destiny apart from our work.

Bad Belief 3: Life should be fair and no inequity should be tolerated. On Planet Earth, nobody is going to escape being treated unfairly, rejected, or disadvantaged in some way at one time or another. It's called *life* in a fallen world. Bad things happen to good people. We can make every effort to change a situation through proper channels—like Martin Luther King Jr., Gandhi, and countless other great men and women have done. However, in the final analysis, wisdom dictates that we sometimes just have to ignore some offenses.

Bad Belief 4: Forgiving a perpetrator is a sign of weakness. Dorner declared, "I have the *strength* and benefits of being unpredictable, unconventional, and unforgiving." Yes, his grudge was indeed a mighty force; however, it propelled him in the wrong direction. It ultimately proved to be his weakness. Only the mentally and morally strong can keep moving forward when offended or treated unfairly, and that requires Divine empowerment. Simmering resentment doesn't strengthen you; it weakens your moral foundation, your ability to be rational, and your ability to succeed.

Bad Belief 5: Revenge is the only viable option. The subject line of Dorner's manifesto read: "Last Resort." How could he possibly believe that revenge killings were his last option to get his name cleared? If he had embraced biblical principles, he would have followed the pattern of Jesus who never fought to protect His name or His reputation. He endured all the hardships and fulfilled His purpose. Today, His name is the name above all names in heaven and on earth. In contrast, what will the masses remember when they hear the name Christopher Dorner?

One of the tragic outcomes of the Dorner case is that many will lose faith in the good, hardworking, honest law enforcement personnel dedicated to serving and protecting—many who are God-fearing and who are my personal friends and family members. The police department's current leadership has acknowledged its troubled past of racism and is making great strides to overcome it.

I pray that neither Dorner's death nor that of his victims has been in vain. I pray that you, dear reader, will remember that when you linger in the Pool of Victimization, your hopes and dreams can shrivel up. We must always believe that God can turn every offense, every disappointment, and every negative situation into something good! He has plans for us to prosper and to bring us to an expected end (Jeremiah 29:11). Let's commit to ridding ourselves of bad beliefs. Let's be transformed by the Word of God and finish well.

2

The Preacher's Son
From Church to Chains

*"If you do not obey the voice of the LORD, but rebel
against the commandment of the LORD, then
the hand of the LORD will be against you."*

1 SAMUEL 12:15

Diane's Story[2]

At nineteen, I had a long distance relationship with a young man in college in Northern California. We dated off and on for two years and continued to date outsiders as well. After only four dates with my new friend Chuck, a handsome 23-year-old fresh out of the navy, I knew we had a special relationship. Around that same time, my college boyfriend sent me a plane ticket to visit him for my birthday. We had a fun time, but my thoughts were with Chuck. The night before I returned home, we had our first and only sexual encounter.

My mom picked me up at the airport and immediately knew I was troubled. I confessed what had happened. Mom was already convinced, as was I, that Chuck was my God-given mate and she was not about to let me mess up my chance to marry him. She devised a well-intentioned but deceitful plan. Chuck was scheduled to come to our home for dinner in two days. Mom convinced me to seduce him so that if I were indeed pregnant, he would automatically believe the child was his. It would be our secret; neither man was ever to know.

I followed her "orders." One week later, my fears were confirmed when I missed my period. I was pregnant. The burden of my deception was too great for my sensitive conscience, so I confessed my pregnancy to both men. Chuck said he already knew I was to become his wife so we married one month later. Though we loved each other and adored our son, Curtis, a tiny seed of unforgiveness lurked in Chuck's heart. He refused to talk about the circumstances of Curtis's conception.

Four years after our marriage, Chuck and I gave our hearts to Jesus. By then, we had two sons. We raised them to know the Lord and to stand on His Word. God was relentless in His pursuit of my heart to forgive my mom for her deceptive tactics and myself for cooperating. I also felt strongly we should have informed Curtis at some point about the circumstances of his conception. Chuck was adamantly opposed to it. This uncertainty about Curtis's birth father became the deadly secret that over forty-five years later still affects my family.

Chuck and I answered the call from God to become ministers. We got ordained and founded a thriving church. We enjoyed working for the Lord and all looked well on the surface. Our sons helped in the nursery, ushered, taught Sunday school, and served in other needed capacities. Nevertheless, something always troubled me about Curtis.

I noticed he always found it hard to let go of an offense. Unforgiveness built up to become a root of bitterness and a seething anger that sometimes tainted his relationships. He increasingly justified any unforgiveness toward me, his teachers, and his classmates. He also became fascinated with violence and violent movies. Although I finally took him to counseling, the sessions became a lost priority to athletic activities after only two visits. I had to forgive myself for not demanding that his counseling take priority in his life and for not bringing up the circumstances of his conception with the counselor.

After 24 years of marriage, Chuck decided he wanted out. He used my deception regarding Curtis's conception as his rationalization that I was not trustworthy. Our divorce was highly publicized as our ministry had gained some notoriety. Many churches who had put out the welcome mat of speaking opportunities for me snatched them up. It was a painful pill to swallow—emotionally and financially.

Four years after the divorce, Curtis, now age 24, married a lovely woman and had two beautiful children. Although they had great times together in the beginning, the marriage turned sour within three years and they divorced. Curtis's problem with unforgiveness escalated. Ten days after the bitter divorce became final, he shot his ex-wife's boyfriend and kidnapped her. Their three-year-old son, two-year-old daughter, and her boyfriend's four-year-old were abandoned at the scene of the crime. They were traumatized and deeply scarred. The boyfriend was paralyzed and unable to function mentally after being shot in the head at close range.

Curtis fled the country after the shooting and temporary kidnapping. He became the focus of a nationwide manhunt. Seven months later, Mexican authorities apprehended him. The

America's Most Wanted television series crew filmed his handover
to US law enforcement. He was charged with attempted murder and kidnapping.

My heart was overwhelmed with questions. How could my
son yield himself to Satan so completely? How could he ignore
the impact his actions would have on his children? Chuck and
I had worked hard to teach and show him how to live according to the Word and to honor God. How could that not give
us some kind of guarantee that he would be a benefit to society
and a blessing to God's kingdom?

The whole ordeal left me grief-stricken and brokenhearted.
Curtis didn't fit the stereotypical profile of a violent criminal.
Chuck and I were saved when Curtis was three years old. He
had the privilege of being raised by a loving mother and father.
He had not been abused or molested. He didn't do drugs or
alcohol; he was never a gang member. Anger and unforgiveness
had simply become his downfall.

Curtis is in prison today serving a life sentence for attempted
murder, kidnapping, and for the 2007 murder of his cellmate,
which added more years to his time. If only he would have
trusted God for the grace to forgive all whom he perceived to
have wronged him, he would probably be a free man today.

This has been a painful experience as I've assumed the role
of a prison mom. Oftentimes, I've had to resist anger at Curtis. I had to forgive him because he knew the Word of God and
chose the enemy's way. I forgave him because, even after being
sentenced, he still ignored my counsel and warnings. I forgave
him for his pride and rebellion.

A major paradigm shift in my thinking came when the Holy Spirit urged me to choose to forgive Curtis for who he has chosen to become and how he has chosen to live his life. This was a better approach than trying to forgive each individual incident of rebellion. Every bad decision he has made is a reflection of his wrong thinking because of who he has become. So I had to embrace that he is not who I want him to be.

Today, Diane, often described as a "grace expert," models and teaches the powerful truth that we must rely upon the grace of God to get us through life and its traumas. As one of her friends, I have witnessed firsthand the joy and quiet confidence she exudes when faced with adversity. She asserts,

> There are times my heart is overwhelmed with the cares of this life. Singing to God is a good way for me to release my faith and access His Grace. When I'm in a hard place, a song may come to mind as I awaken or at some time during the day. If I sing it out loud to the Lord, I can sense faith arise and grace fill my mind. [3]

3

A Wife's Revenge
What's Good for the Goose Is
Good for the Gander

Marriage is honorable among all, and the bed undefiled;
but fornicators and adulterers God will judge.

HEBREWS 13:4

Helen's Story

I lived with my crack-addicted, verbally and physically abusive mother the first 14 years of my life. She kicked me out when I told her I wanted to live with my dad. I had long grown weary of the abuse and the constant hunger. During the 4 years I lived with my dad and my stepmother, I rarely saw him. He never really spoke to me other than to express disappointment with my grades.

Upon graduation I went to live with my aunt in Georgia. I was very shy and introverted. I attended a very strict Pentecostal church. At age 21, I met and married John, an obese introvert who topped the scales at 350 pounds. For the most part, we got along. We didn't fight much. He came home every night, he didn't drink, and he didn't hit me. So for 12 years, it was a tolerable marriage.

One day John expressed his desire to go to nursing school so he could make more money. I supported him, thinking I was being a good wife. He quit his job as a probation officer, and I took on a second job. I worked nights and frequently stayed up 24 hours straight to go to the second job and take care of our two kids.

The nursing school curriculum required the students to work in study groups, which John initially resisted. Oddly, the next semester he seemed to be unable to pull himself away from his group. During this time, he lost 160 pounds, dropping down to 200. Then, I learned he was having an affair.

Initially, he was remorseful about it—or at least he pretended to be since he was a jobless full-time student. I was devastated. From his emails and texts, it appeared he loved the other woman. He never seemed to care about what was going on with me. I was in an emotional quandary. My weight plummeted; I lost 30 pounds in one month.

I became numb and angry. I was angry with God, myself, and John. Late one night I woke up from a horrible dream in which he was kissing a girl. I noted that John was sleeping peacefully. I resented that. I said to the Lord, "Well, it seems no one ever has to pay for hurting me. So looks like it's everyman for himself now." In my heart, I walked away from God at that moment. I decided I would engage in every activity I'd resisted over the years because it was a sin.

One day, when I was downloading music from the Internet, an advertisement for an X-rated site popped up. I opened it. I eventually became a member of the site, met up with random people, and had random sex—until I finally was caught. By then, I was so numb I didn't care. I didn't deny it nor did I attempt to make excuses.

John kicked me out the night he found out. He now felt it was his job to punish me for my wrongdoing. For days, he wouldn't talk to me and I slept on the couch; when we did talk, we fought. We decided to dissolve the marriage five months after my sin was discovered.

The judge ordered me to leave the house and pay John $1,200 per month for child support. For 16 months, I saw my two girls only every other weekend and every other Wednesday. This was a very painful period. I came to the end of myself and realized I couldn't deal with the pain, disappointment, and hurt. I desperately needed God.

The day the judge told me I had to leave the house, I went to a hotel and pigged out on a bag of junk food. Then, I decided to write God a brief letter.

> Father God, I believe there is a battle going on in
> the heavenlies for me. If You are there, if You are
> real, please get me out of this mess I created. I've
> done wrong, but I will give You my life if You show
> me Yourself.

Before this "coming to Jesus" moment, I'd merely heard about God. I went to church but I never had a life-changing experience with Him. I decided to dedicate myself to God while I was away from the life I once knew—stripped of everything. I prayed and read the Bible. I prayed so much I would wake in my sleep praying.

By the time it was all over, God had restored everything: primary custody of the children, the house, the cars, everything. Life hasn't been easy post-divorce. I still work two jobs and have a record time of staying awake for almost 36 hours. I wouldn't trade the peace and joy I have today for the world. I forgive because today I know God for myself; He showed up in my life when I needed Him the most.

It took a while for me to forgive myself for the part I played in the whole ordeal. But once I got it in my head that God had forgiven me, nothing my ex-husband or anyone else said could cause me to put my head down in shame.

I had to forgive John so that God would forgive me. Recently, I've realized I have indeed forgiven him because neither he nor his offense is the first thing on my mind when I awaken each day. I don't feel rage when I think of him. I pray for him as the Lord brings him to mind.

We had married at a young age and, in retrospect, neither of us had any idea what true marriage was nor how to really love another person. As we grew up, we grew apart. I was no longer introverted and shy; he stayed introverted. We had very different ideas how we should raise our kids, and we were unequally yoked spiritually.

I am free now. I'm free to live, love, and worship. People frequently compliment my smile. I believe it comes from a God-given inner peace and the joy in my heart.

4

Samson Versus the Philistines
A Vicious Cycle of Wrongs and Retaliation

"An eye for an eye will only make the whole world blind."

Mahatma Gandhi

The Israelites, God's chosen people, just couldn't seem to stop sinning. Time and again, they disobeyed His commands and found themselves in the hands of their enemies. True to His merciful character, God would raise up a leader to deliver them.

Meet Samson. He judged Israel for 20 years. I'll let him tell you his story, quoting him directly in most instances or paraphrasing the biblical narrative for clarity. You may first want to familiarize yourself with the account by reading Judges 13–16.

Samson's Story

My story begins with my miraculous birth to a barren couple. An angel of the Lord appeared to my parents and promised they'd have a son. He instructed them that I was to be a Nazirite, separated for special service all the days of my life and that I was never to cut my hair. Further, the angel promised that I would begin to deliver the Israelites from the rule of the mighty Philistines. The Spirit of God began to move upon me early in life.

One day I went down to the city of Timnah, and a young Philistine woman captured my attention. As was the custom, I asked my parents to arrange for me to marry her. They balked.

"Isn't there an acceptable woman among your relatives or among all our people? Must you go to the uncircumcised Philistines to get a wife?" I was persistent and they finally relented. Of course, neither they nor I knew God was orchestrating the whole thing because He was laying the groundwork for the defeat of the Philistines.

My parents and I headed to Timnah to negotiate the marriage terms. I was making a quick side excursion alone through the vineyards when a young lion came roaring at me out of nowhere. I had no weapon or anything to defend myself. The Spirit of the Lord came upon me, and I tore the lion apart with my bare hands. I didn't tell my mother or father about the incident. Sometime later, when I went back to get married, I turned aside to look at the lion's carcass. It was covered with a swarm of bees and lots of honey. I scooped out some honey with my hands and ate it. When I rejoined my parents, I gave them some too. Of course, I didn't tell them where it had come from.

Well, the wedding was a blast. Thirty young Philistine men were invited to be my companions, and during the festivities, I posed a riddle to them: "'Out of the eater, something to eat; out of the strong, something sweet.' If you can give me the answer to my riddle within the seven days of the feast, I will give you thirty linen garments and thirty sets of clothes. If you can't tell me the answer, you must give me thirty linen garments and thirty sets of clothes."

When they could not give the answer by the fourth day, they went to my wife and threatened to burn her and her father alive in their house if she didn't find a way to get the answer from me. She came to me in tears, "You hate me! You don't really love me.

You've given my people a riddle, but you haven't told me the answer." She cried the whole seven days of the feast. I couldn't stand the nagging, so on the seventh day, I finally told her.

When on the last day of the feast the men of the town gave me the correct answer to the riddle, I knew right away they'd gotten it from her because I hadn't told anyone else. I was livid! Then the Spirit of the Lord came upon me in power. I went down to the city of Ashkelon, struck down thirty of their men, stripped them of their belongings, and gave their clothes to those who had explained the riddle. Then I stomped off to my father's house, leaving my wife behind.

This action began a cycle of offenses and retaliation between the Philistines and me.

When I went back to visit my wife sometime later, my father-in-law said he had given her to one of the wedding companions because he thought I hated her and would never return. This made me very angry. To exact revenge on the Philistines, I went out, caught three hundred foxes, and tied them tail to tail in pairs. I then fastened a torch to every pair of tails, lit the torches, and let the foxes loose in the standing grain. They burned up the grain, the vineyards, and the olive groves.

This really infuriated the Philistines when they learned I was the culprit. So they went up and burned my wife and her father to death. Well, I wasn't going to let them off with that! I was going to avenge this wrong for sure. I attacked them viciously and slaughtered many of them. Then I went out and hid in a cave.

But the Philistines were as committed to payback as I was. They prepared to attack my people if they didn't turn me over to them. A fearful and frustrated 3000-man contingent from the tribe of Judah came to appeal to me to turn myself in.

"Don't you realize that the Philistines are rulers over us? What have you done to us?"

I surrendered peacefully and allowed them to bind me with two new ropes; then we headed out to the place where they would turn me in. As we approached our destination, the Philistines came toward me shouting. The Spirit of the Lord came upon me in power. I flexed and popped those ropes like they were thin threads. I grabbed the fresh jawbone of a donkey and struck down 1000 men—making a donkey of all of them.

I knew this was not the end of our vicious cycle of offenses and retaliation.

Sometime later, I fell in love with a woman named Delilah. The rulers of the Philistines went to her and said, "See if you can lure him into showing you the secret of his great strength and how we can overpower him so we may tie him up and subdue him. Each one of us will give you eleven hundred shekels of silver."

So Delilah started pestering me for the secret to my strength. I lied to her three times about the various sources of my great strength. She tested me with each one of them and each time I overcame her efforts to subdue me. She almost nagged me to death, telling me that I couldn't possibly love her if I wouldn't share my heart. I finally told her everything:

"No razor has ever been used on my head," I said, "because I have been a Nazirite set apart to God since birth. If my head were shaved, my strength would leave me, and I would become as weak as any other man."

Well, that did it. When I went to sleep, she had my head shaved. All my strength left me. Then the Philistines seized me, gouged out my eyes, and bound me with shackles. They sent me to grind in the prison. The cycle of revenge had cost me my strength, my sight, and my freedom.

After a while, my hair began to grow back. One day, the Philistine rulers decided to put on a celebration to thank their god for delivering me into their hands. They sent for me to perform for them, to make sport of me.

The place was packed. All the rulers were there; over 3000 men and women joined in my humiliation. I'm sure Delilah was in the crowd also. I asked the servant who'd guided me into the arena to put me where I could feel the pillars that supported the temple that I may lean against them.

Then I prayed to the Lord, "O Sovereign Lord, remember me. O God, please strengthen me just once more, and let me with one blow get revenge on the Philistines for my two eyes." Then I reached toward the two central pillars on which the temple stood. Bracing myself against them, my right hand on the one and my left hand on the other, I said, "Let me die with the Philistines!" Then I pushed with all my might, and down came the temple on the rulers and all the people in it. Thus, I killed more when I died than while I lived.

What's the moral of this story? There is no happy ending to revenge. However, God is merciful and will still hear our prayers when we call upon Him out of a contrite heart.

5

Is Revenge Really Sweet?

"Weak people revenge, strong people forgive,
and intelligent people ignore."

UNKNOWN

Several years ago, a man sped out of a side street and broadsided my car near a busy intersection. Shaken but grateful that I wasn't injured, I pulled over to exchange insurance information with him. Rather than following suit, he backed his car up quickly and took off.

I was furious; I didn't even get his license number. I tried to catch him, but he drove much too fast. I don't know what I would have done had I caught up with him, but I remember thinking, *I wish I had a stun gun or something that would inflict severe pain on him without killing him.*

Avenging a wrong seems to be entrenched in our carnal nature. Sometimes I feel so un-Christian because of the delight I get from seeing the bad guys in movies finally get what they deserve—even at the hands of a revengeful vigilante versus the established judicial process. Some movies bring out the worst in us.

But who doesn't like to see justice served? Why, it's the very reason people adore Spiderman, Batman, Superman, Thor, and all the other superheroes: they make sure the menaces to society get their just deserts.

Then along comes Jesus, the greatest superhero of all times. He tells us to forgive an offender and to leave the payback to Him. It's no wonder that Christians and non-Christians struggle with this concept. It is tantamount to a command to run backward; it simply goes against our *natural* inclination. That's why I'm so grateful for the grace of God that motivates and empowers God's children to walk in the Spirit so that we will not fulfill the desires of our sinful nature (see Galatians 5:16).

Ironically, when we retaliate (verbally or physically) or attempt to exact revenge in any form, the satisfaction is only fleeting—like when the bad driver cuts you off and you honk your horn in protest. Avenging a wrong just won't give you the lasting satisfaction, the peace, or the closure you thought it would.

Colgate University psychologist Kevin Carlsmith and his colleagues conducted three studies that demonstrated that revenge, rather than being sweet, made those who took part in the study less happy and increased their anger. These researchers found that one reason for this is that people who punish continue to dwell on the offender, whereas those who do not punish move on and think less about the offender.[4]

When a Christian seeks revenge, he is in essence saying, "God, I don't trust You to avenge the wrong done against me. I'd better take matters into my own hands." For those who chose not to retaliate, even the alternative coping strategies often fail. For example, many mental health professionals recommend writing a letter to the offender, letting all the anger out but not mailing it, or cutting up the person's photo and flushing it down the toilet.

I prefer the old-school way set forth in 2 Corinthian 10:5: "Casting down arguments, and every high thing that exalts itself against the knowledge of God, bringing every thought into captivity to the obedience of Christ." I believe in calling upon the Holy Spirit to help me cast down every thought of retaliation because such thinking rises up against what the Word of God says about His promise to avenge every wrong. Yes, I realize even the thought of revenge can bring some *temporary* satisfaction. But, why luxuriate in thoughts that are contrary to His will and His way?

To triumph over vengeful thoughts, always stop and think through the consequences of and positive alternatives to your proposed actions:

- What will this action cost me personally (potential job loss, jail time, loss of particular relationships, loss of respect)?

- What impact will it have on those who love me (heartbreak, embarrassment, disappointment, loss of social standing)?

- Will it undo the damage done by the perpetrator? (Nope!)

- Is there an opportunity to achieve justice under the law? (Be honest here. Is justice your *true* objective, or are you driven by anger and a need to see the offender suffer pain? Get real about your motivation.)

- Do I have all the facts surrounding this situation, or

should I wait to obtain more information directly
from the offender or witnesses?

- Is there any way I can respond to this hurt that will
  have a long-term positive impact, such as voicing
  my forgiveness, speaking out against certain crimes,
  working to change laws, starting a nonprofit organi-
  zation? (For example, the powerful Mothers Against
  Drunk Drivers (www.madd.org) was borne out
  of pain over the loss of loved ones at the hands of
  drunken drivers.)

One of the best examples in the Bible of someone deter-
mined to avenge a wrong but stopping dead in his tracks to consider the consequences is found in 1 Samuel 25. When David
was fleeing the wrath of Saul, he and his men befriended and
protected the herdsmen of Nabal, a rich but surly landowner.
Assuming Nabal valued such protection, David sent a few of his
men to ask him for food for his hungry crew. Nabal insulted the
men and sent them away. David was so enraged, he vowed to
kill every person in Nabal's household. However, when Nabal's
beautiful and wise wife, Abigail, heard about the incident, she
put a huge care package together, headed out, and intercepted
David en route to her home. Her rational and passionate argu-
ment regarding the consequences of David's intended actions
averted a crisis:

- Ignore a fool; Nabal is a fool, as his name indicates
  (v. 25).

- By not taking vengeance into your own hands,
  God's going to curse all your enemies (v. 26).

- God's going to reward you with a lasting dynasty
  (v. 28).

- Even though you are chased by Saul, your life is safe
  and secure in God (v. 29).

- When you become the leader of Israel, you don't
  want Nabal's death to be a blemish on your record
  nor do you want needless bloodshed and vengeance
  on your conscious (vv. 30-31).

After such a powerful intervention, David triumphed over
his anger and abandoned all thoughts of revenge:

> David said to Abigail, "Praise be to the LORD, the
> God of Israel, who has sent you today to meet me.
> May you be blessed for your good judgment and
> for keeping me from bloodshed this day and from
> avenging myself with my own hands" (vv. 32-33
> NIV).

Yes, dear reader, carrying out revenge brings little satisfaction
and will most likely create more problems and suffering. So stop,
think, and pray before you act.

Part 2

Stories of Forgiveness

6

Forgiving God
When the Divine Disappoints

How long, O LORD? Will You forget me forever?
How long will You hide Your face from me?

PSALM 13:1

After being broadsided by tragedy, a betrayal, a death, or having to endure a prolonged period of physical or emotional pain, it's not unusual to end up feeling forsaken—and angry at God. Let's face it. Some of the situations He allows us to experience are just downright infuriating. As we stew in our anger over them, we wrestle with the reality that He had the power to prevent or fix any situation, but instead allowed a path that caused us grief. Why would a loving Father do that? I suspect we've all asked that question at some point in our lives.

Our anger can keep us away from God when we need Him the most. One pastor said that church members would occasionally confess they'd stopped attending services because they were angry at God. Most of the time they were ashamed of their feelings, but they weren't willing to forgive Him. Frustrated and deflated in their faith, they were stuck in bewilderment. Thankfully, many people of faith who have been angry at God learned that forgiving their Creator restores them to a right relationship with Him and revives their faith.

Christine was one of those people. Although she and her

sister, Chelsea, weren't close growing up, as adults they became best friends.

Chelsea moved to another state with her husband, Brian. Later, she began having health issues that puzzled her doctors. After months of tests, they discovered she had a rare disease that affected her physically and mentally. The stress of her disease destroyed Chelsea's marriage. Brian walked out, leaving her to raise their three daughters alone. Christine, who had recently ended a relationship herself, moved across country to take care of Chelsea and her children.

Chelsea held on for seven years. There were numerous hospitalizations and frightening mental breakdowns. She suffered terribly, and then one summer day, she died at home with her family at her bedside.

Christine had always been a woman of faith, but she didn't understand why God would allow her sister to suffer so much and take her away from her school-age children. She went through the motions of serving God for almost a decade, going to church, praying—all the things Christians are supposed to do—to be a role model for her own children. Deep within, however, she harbored anger at God—until the Holy Spirit removed the scales from her eyes.

"One day I realized that God was still doing wonderful things in my life," Christine said. "The doctors caught my mother's cancer early, and now she was healed. My children were becoming wonderful people because of their faith. I didn't understand why Chelsea had to suffer, but I began to see that God was still working in my life."

Christine decided to forgive God.

"Finally, I'm free," she said.

So, why do we get angry at God? Because we try to make sense of the world and God with our limited human thinking. We have our own ideas and expectations as to how a problem or situation should be resolved. However, *God always has a higher purpose.*

> "For my thoughts are not your thoughts,
>   neither are your ways my ways,"
>   declares the LORD.
> "As the heavens are *higher* than the earth,
>   so are my ways *higher* than your ways
>   and my thoughts than your thoughts."
>   (Isaiah 55:8-9 NIV)

We may never totally comprehend why God allows us to experience certain difficulties. We need to just settle this fact in our hearts. We also need to settle the truth that our Lord and Savior suffered on the cross for our salvation, and when we suffer, He suffers along with us. Jesus tells us to take up our cross—not one we conveniently choose—and follow Him. He never promises that our life as Christians will be easy or carefree. But He does promise something greater—to be with us during our sorrows and to give us eternal life that is free from pain, suffering, and injustice.

Scripture shows us that being angry or frustrated with God is common in people of faith. Several of the psalms reveal the psalmists' anguish and pain. However, despite their woes, they held on to their faith. They quickly shifted their focus from the circumstances they were enduring to the good that God has provided:

I say to God my Rock,
  "Why have you forgotten me?
Why must I go about mourning,
  oppressed by the enemy?"
My bones suffer mortal agony
  as my foes taunt me,
saying to me all day long,
  "Where is your God?"
Why, my soul, are you downcast?
  Why so disturbed within me?
Put your hope in God,
  for I will yet praise him,
  my Savior and my God.
                    (Psalm 42:9-11 NIV)

Notice the psalmist's self-talk. He speaks to his own soul (his mind, will, and emotions), encouraging himself to put his hope in God despite the circumstances.

Even Job, after losing his wealth, his health, and his children, declared, "Though He slay me, yet will I trust Him. *Even so, I will defend my own ways before Him*" (Job 13:15). In essence, what he was saying was, "I trust God, but I want to express that I do not deserve what's happening to me." (He goes on to do so in Job 31, citing a litany of his righteous acts.)

Yes, folks, we can freely release all our emotions before Him. We do it through prayer, our most powerful tool for unlocking the door to forgiveness. Ironically, we need God's empowering grace to help us to forgive Him. And, no, He won't strike us dead for being angry with Him. *The only real danger is holding on to the anger and allowing it to separate us from our fellowship with Him.*

So forget about flowery prayers or praying what we think He wants to hear. God already knows what's in our heart, so we can pour it all out before Him. He is big enough to handle every negative emotion. He became fully human in Jesus Christ to experience our struggles right alongside us. We are never, ever left alone. God is always faithful no matter what. "Do not be afraid or discouraged, for the LORD will personally go ahead of you. He will be with you; he will neither fail you nor abandon you" (Deuteronomy 31:8 NLT).

Lessons learned

In our darkest hour and amid the worst of circumstances, the Lord is with us whether we *feel* His presence or not. To move toward forgiving Him, we must:

- Pour out our true feelings in prayer.

- Be honest about what we feel God did "wrong." Consider that we may be directing anger toward Him that we feel toward ourselves or another person responsible for our pain.

- As an act of faith, we must declare our trust in His wisdom and Divine choices. Perhaps one day we will understand and say as Job did: "I take back everything I said, and I sit in dust and ashes to show my repentance" (Job 42:6 NLT).

- Acknowledge and express gratitude for His continued blessings.

7

Forgiving Yourself
Letting Go of Guilt

*"I, even I, am he who blots out
your transgressions, for my own sake,
and remembers your sins no more."*

ISAIAH 43:25 NIV

"Jasper was an alcoholic most of his life and had destroyed his liver," the hospital chaplain said. "With God's help he quit drinking, but his health continued to decline."

Chaplain Greg first saw Jasper two days after he nearly died from liver disease. His doctor had finally approved him for a transplant, but for several reasons, his odds of getting a match were low. Undaunted, Jasper had confidently proclaimed, "God wants me to live to witness His grace in forgiveness."

Greg marveled that Jasper refused to beat himself up like most people who have destroyed their lives through drinking or drugs. "Jasper told me that once he stopped drinking, he forgave himself," Greg said. "He also asked forgiveness from his family and worked to reconcile his relationship with his ex-wife and children."

Against all the odds, Jasper remained hopeful that he would receive a liver. His recommitment to God had stirred his faith— and God honored it. Jasper survived the extremely risky surgery and experienced a quick recovery.

"I firmly believe that forgiving himself gave Jasper the hope and strength he needed to survive," Greg said. "He is a prime example of what happens when you accept God's forgiveness."

Victor's story was the opposite of Jasper's. He was a ladies' man until he was 40 years old. No matter where he went, women were captivated by his charm, good looks, and magnetic personality. As he approached 45, he met and fell in love with Ornie, a beautiful, hard-working, no-nonsense woman with strong relational boundaries. She informed him in clear terms that cheating with other women would be a deal breaker. They lived together for a few years. Then one day, while praying for a breakthrough in a potential business venture, Victor had an encounter with God.

"God showed me that my life was never going to get on track unless I served Him," he said. "I must marry Ornie if I'm to be blessed and have peace of mind."

Victor went on a three-day fast and decided to obey God. He and Ornie had a beautiful wedding. However, five years later, his emotional world started to crumble as Satan launched one of his most powerful weapons: a guilt missile. Victor could not handle the overwhelming remorse he felt as he recalled the havoc he had wreaked in the lives of various women over the past 20 years: the abortions he'd insisted upon, his two-timing ways that had driven a few to the brink of suicide, and even the physical abuse he had perpetrated against some.

Although he had grown up in a church-going family, he did not have a solid foundation in the Word of God. He often sought refuge in alcohol. Though I explained it to him repeatedly, he could not fathom that God would actually forgive him and wipe his slate clean. He felt he deserved punishment.

Oddly, Satan's assault came when Victor was on the brink of closing a long-awaited multimillion-dollar business deal. Suddenly, it meant nothing to him. He couldn't bring himself to focus on the few glitches that he needed to resolve in order to complete the deal. He lost a significant amount of weight in just a few weeks.

Recently, I challenged Victor to counter the guilty thoughts by declaring throughout each day, based on John 8:36: "Jesus Christ has set me free; therefore, I am free indeed!" I see a glimmer of hope. His appetite has returned. He is saturating his mind with the Word of God and listening to powerful sermons on self-forgiveness.

Dear friend, no sin you commit is too big or too bad to be forgiven. The apostle Paul, looking back on his sin of severely persecuting early Christians, boldly declared that rather than staying stuck in his painful history, he was choosing to put it behind him: "I focus on this one thing: Forgetting the past and looking forward to what lies ahead, I press on to reach the end of the race and receive the heavenly prize for which God, through Christ Jesus, is calling us" (Philippians 3:13-14 NLT). Paul was remorseful and *hopeful*. He decided to maximize the rest of his life and became an ambassador for the Lord. He refocused his passion, preached and suffered for the gospel, and wrote over half the books in the New Testament.

In contrast, Judas—who had enjoyed a one-on-one relationship with Christ as a member of the original twelve hand-selected disciples—betrayed Jesus for 30 pieces of silver. He was remorseful but *hopeless*. All he had to do was confess his sin and ask for forgiveness. Instead, his guilt drove him to commit suicide (see Matthew 27:1-5).

What about you? Are you wallowing in condemnation over a past action? Do you realize that whatever sin you committed, it did not catch God by surprise? Yes, He knew you were going to do it. That's why He put a plan in place over 2000 years ago for your redemption. "If we confess our sins, He is faithful and just to forgive us our sins and to cleanse us from all unrighteousness" (1 John 1:9). It's time to cash in on that promise.

Lessons learned

Moving toward self-forgiveness requires:

- Recognizing that God's grace is already at work within you. You are acknowledging your wrongdoing rather than justifying or excusing it. You are calling your unrighteousness exactly what God calls it—sin!

- Confessing your sin before the Lord. Once is enough. No need to keep confessing it. He grants forgiveness the *first* time that you mean it. You must now give yourself permission to stop sacrificing your peace of mind on the altar of condemnation. "And when sins have been forgiven, there is no need to offer any more sacrifices" (Hebrews 10:18 NLT).

- Confessing your sin to someone you know who exercises godly wisdom—your pastor, priest, a counselor, or a longtime trusted friend. "Confess your sins to each other and pray for each other so that you may be healed. The earnest prayer of a righteous person has great power and produces wonderful results" (James 5:16 NLT). Others often have a different perspective and can help you sort out your feelings, perhaps find the lesson learned, and offer practical ideas and strategies for moving forward.

- Asking your victim for forgiveness. Humility is critical here. Own all your bad behavior without blaming anyone else—especially the victim. Be truly repentant.

- Searching for ways to make restitution, if possible. If you stole something, pay back what you owe. If you hurt someone, apologize sincerely. She may choose not to forgive you; it's her prerogative. You are not responsible for anyone's response; your goal is simply to do the right thing. There is freedom in doing that.

- Repenting. Ask for God's help (and that of others—including a professional, if necessary) to turn your back on your sin.

- Receiving His forgiveness. Declare daily: "Jesus Christ has set me free; therefore, I am free indeed!"

Forgiving Your Parents
Triumphing Over Expectations

*"Honor your father and your mother, that your days may be
long upon the land which the Lord your God is giving you."*

Exodus 20:12

Barbara's Story

I had read Bible verses on forgiveness repeatedly, but for the first
year that I followed the Lord, I didn't see the benefits to myself.
I felt that forgiving a person made it okay for him or her to hurt
me, and that I was giving up my rights as a human being. I
made a lot of excuses, such as, "Oh, I tried, but the anger keeps
coming back." "Well, I'm not Jesus, and you don't know what
this person did to me." I told myself, *God just has to understand
what I've been through.*

But one fine spring day, at a bus stop, the Holy Spirit showed
me how to let go and move on.

In the middle of the week at my call-center job, my boss dismissed me early due to the low volume of incoming calls. After
walking several blocks to my bus stop, I noticed the bench was
unoccupied, flanked by one scraggly oak tree. I had obviously
missed the bus as there were usually at least a dozen people waiting there.

Standing there alone made me think of my loneliness in life,
and how my parents had always made me feel alienated from

the rest of the family. They had never gotten over their disappointment that I was born a girl, and my life with them just went downhill from there. They made me feel that I would never amount to anything in life, and at that moment, while I was feeling sorry for myself because I was missing half-a-day's pay at a lousy job that I hated, I believed them. My heart had been shattered by their ill-treatment from very early on, and then broken by others for over 47 years. Tears poured from my eyes. I silently prayed, *Lord, I don't want to live this way. If I have to spend another 40 years with this pain in my heart, then I wish You'd just take me now. I can't stand this anymore.*

Just then, a Bible verse I'd always had a problem accepting came to mind: "He who finds his life will lose it, and he who loses his life for My sake will find it" (Matthew 10:39). I never understood that verse; it sounded as though the only way to get to heaven was to be martyred. After all I'd been through, I really hated that thought. I whispered, "Lord, what now? Do I have to get my head chopped off before I'm okay?" And the Spirit spoke to my heart, "Forgive."

I had heard it said that forgiveness is a little death, a dying to yourself. You have to give up your right to be angry at someone in order to let go of the offense or the pain, and that means surrendering a part of yourself, a part of your life. The Spirit reminded me that not only were all of my sins covered, but that Christ shed His blood for everyone else's sins also—whether everyone embraced that forgiveness or not. I needed to experience that "little death" in order to lose the resentment I was dragging around like a heavy weight. This was a moment of truth that I wasn't expecting.

I didn't know how to forgive. No one in my dysfunctional life had ever forgiven me for anything I'd done wrong, and I'd never seen anyone forgive others. I prayed, *Lord, I'm willing, but I don't know how. You have to do it for me.* And He did! When I surrendered my right to hate my parents for the horrible way they had made me feel, God lifted the heavy burden of hating them from my heart. He also lifted the burden of feeling like a failure.

When I was finished praying, I felt physically lighter. That was amazing because I weighed more than 300 pounds. I stopped crying then and saw pure, clear sunlight through the scrawny oak tree. Five minutes beforehand, all I had heard was traffic and horns honking, but suddenly I heard birds singing above me.

These three things—lightness of spirit, the beautiful sunlight, and the singing birds—were all little bits of joy that God had wanted to lavish on me, but I was blocking those blessings by carrying around my anger. Before the bus came, I started quietly singing one of my favorite praise songs, and I continued to hum it quietly on the bus ride home. I went from weeping to singing!

I still struggle with forgiveness because there's a lot in my past to forgive. Sometimes the same issues keep popping up for me, but I keep putting them under the blood of Christ, just as the Spirit showed me to do at that bus stop. The times in my life when I start nurturing resentment and victimization are the times I have been the most depressed, even suicidal. But when I stop and remember who I really am in Christ and what He requires of me to follow Him, I am able to let go of the pain and stop believing that I'm damaged beyond repair.

I've found that forgiveness is a matter of whom I choose to believe. Do I believe I'm struggling against what human beings have done to me? If so, I'm not seeing the truth. Ephesians 6:12 tells me that my struggle is not against flesh and blood, but against "spiritual forces of evil" (NIV). No doubt, Satan motivated my parents to mistreat me in the first place. Forgiving my parents benefits me emotionally because I'm living in the truth of God's Word and able to pinpoint the true enemy in my life. I'm no longer struggling uselessly against other people, but rather protecting myself by recognizing the true source of my pain. Even though my parents are deceased, I have compassion in my heart for the struggles and the pain they went through.

Lessons learned

- Forgiveness allows me to walk in the light of Romans 12:2—to be transformed by the renewing of my mind.

- Forgiveness liberates me to dwell on whatever is true, honorable, pure, lovely, positive, excellent, and praiseworthy (Philippians 4:8), instead of being stuck in whatever is hurtful, negative, degrading, and shameful.

- Forgiveness enables me to choose life.

9

Forgiving Your Adoptive Parents
Truth Revealed

*"And you shall know the truth, and the
truth shall make you free."*

JOHN 8:32

Sean was adopted at birth, but didn't know it until his adopted parents told him when he was eight. They had never intended to tell him at all, but a family member let the cat out of the bag and his parents had no choice but to tell him the truth.

"I felt so relieved," Sean said. "I knew there was something wrong, but I didn't know what it was. Once I found out I was adopted, it all made sense."

Unfortunately, Sean's adoptive parents' deception didn't stop there. Even well into his adulthood, they told him they knew nothing about his birth parents. Sean felt like something didn't add up.

"When I was 45, my grandmother died, and I got her Bible," he said. "I was looking through the clippings and other stuff she had saved in between the pages and found a letter." Sean's heart sank as he read the words on the page. "I found out I was the birth son of my mother's cousin Doris."

Sean was furious about his adoptive parents withholding the truth. Doris had passed away several years before, and Sean felt his parents had denied him the opportunity to have a mother/

son relationship with her. Plus there was no clue who his birth father was.

Sean confronted his parents with the letter and asked for an explanation. "My father was furious," he said. "He told me I shouldn't be meddling in that business. I couldn't believe he didn't understand that it *was* my business. My mother started to cry and told me they were trying to protect me from getting hurt." Doris had been involved in gang activity and drug dealing. Sean's parents were afraid that even as an adult, he may be hurt if he started to look for the truth about his birth.

"I'd been lied to my whole life," he said. "I felt like I couldn't trust anybody."

It was months before Sean could talk to his parents again. He underwent counseling with his pastor and learned to try to see things from their perspective. He began to realize that his parents were plagued with immobilizing fear. They couldn't let go of him, to let God take care of him, even after he became an adult. That realization, which came to him in prayer, helped him to move toward forgiving his parents.

When God commands us to forgive, there are no exceptions or exemptions. Adoptive parents are humans born in sin. They need the same level of mercy and compassion as any other sinner or fallible human.

Adoptive parents have lots of fears, and understandably so. There are a lot of unknowns with adoption, and we all tend to fear what we can't control. If you were adopted, your parents had the courage to choose you, despite many unknowns about your conception and the mental, social, or physical history of your birth parents. Give 'em a break. If you found out they were deceptive out of a desire to protect you, think of the pain they must have experienced knowing they were withholding a secret from someone they loved—you.

Maybe now it's time to offer the same intercessory prayer Jesus prayed on the cross: "Father, forgive them, for they do not know what they do" (Luke 23:34).

It's often easier to forgive parents when we try to see things from their perspective. Bridget was able to forgive her parents and even restore her relationship with them in spite of beatings from her father throughout her childhood.

"My dad is mentally ill and never got treatment," she said. "My mom is terrified of him. After I grew up and moved out, I started to feel more pity for them than anything else." She also said prayer was critical. "I think my years of prayer to forgive my parents sort of reshaped my thoughts. And becoming a parent myself helped too. I realized that even though I never beat my children, I was never going to be the perfect mother. I did the best I could and I know my parents did the best they could."

Most parents learn how to raise their children from their own parents. Even if they know that lying, beating, or sexually abusing their children is wrong, they may find it impossible to stop without help. And others simply don't know what they do.

As with any other person, you can forgive your parents and still choose not to have a relationship with them. You can honor the fact that they gave you life, but you don't have to put yourself back into an abusive situation. Forgiving your parents will release you from your hurts and regrets and allow you to put yourself on the path to healing instead of perpetuating the poor parenting on your own children.

Adult children who have suffered abuse from their fathers sometimes find it helpful to think about God in other ways than as Father. There are lots of names for God in the Bible, and substituting *Creator*, *Healer*, or *Protector* for *Father* may help in the healing process.

Lessons learned

You can move past the hurts you've received from your parents and use that experience to become a better parent yourself. Here are some steps to take toward forgiveness:

- Pray for the willingness to forgive.

- Seek first to understand. Perhaps your parent was a victim of poor parenting skills of their own parents. Commit to breaking the cycle.

- If *Father* language in Scripture interferes with your ability to read the Bible or pray, substitute another name for God until you can forgive your earthly father.

10

Forgiving a Runaway Father

Even if my father and mother abandon me,
the LORD will hold me close.

PSALM 27:10 NLT

Joanie's Story

Twenty-seven years of pent-up emotions released themselves as we sat in a corner booth at the Fish Market. It was brunch time on Father's Day 1999, and the place was packed. The late morning sun was streaming in through the window as I watched the ice in our glasses twinkle in the rays. Atlanta was beautiful that day. All eyes were upon my dad and me as we held hands across the table. He was a distinguished, handsome man in a light-gray suit. His curly white hair and bright blue eyes were a beautiful contrast. There was no denying that I was his daughter with my curly brown hair and blue eyes.

"Let me explain." As he said it, his eyes welled up with tears and he gripped my hands harder.

This was my opportunity to say all the things I had practiced in the mirror for the past 11 years. I wanted so badly to tell him how angry I had been growing up without him in my life. The need to tell him about every Christmas or birthday he missed was overwhelming. I wanted to defend my mother because she'd struggled so hard to support us. As I looked at him sitting across from me, I could tell he was financially stable; his car parked outside confirmed it. I thought about all the times my mom had to work overtime just to buy us a bag of groceries and how, at one point in our lives, she had to get on food stamps but was too embarrassed to go inside the market to use them. She'd sent me in instead. There were tons of pictures I wanted to show him where my pants were too short because Mom didn't have the money to buy me new ones.

"Please, listen to me." He squeezed my hands as the tears flowed down his cheeks.

The memory of sitting in my mom's bedroom at age 16 and reading her diaries popped into my head. That was the day I learned about my father and how he had been married when they met. My mom was just a side item to him. When she got pregnant with me, he disappeared. He quit his job at the hospital and left town.

I grew up my entire life knowing only his name. For 11 years I looked his name up in every phonebook in every town I landed. I wanted to tell him how many times I had been cussed out because I'd asked some man if he knew my mom and had a daughter back in Alabama. Maybe I could tell him about the two-hour drive I took by myself to knock on the door of a strange man with the same name, but instead of being nice, the man tried to lure me inside to hurt me. I wondered if he would like to hear about how I had started drinking and doing drugs at age 13 because of all the pain I was feeling and how I hadn't stopped until just a couple of years ago.

"I need to tell you what happened." His tears were coming hard and he was sobbing loudly.

It was odd that he felt the desire to tell me so badly about how he'd screwed up and how much remorse he felt. I wondered if he had practiced in the mirror all these years what he would say to me if we were ever face-to-face. It was only because God had led me to Atlanta for a job opportunity that I found myself sitting in a hotel the night before. I must have picked up the Atlanta phone book four times before I finally decided to call. I wanted to tell him how I almost didn't call, and then when I did, how much I wanted to hang up. A part of me wanted to yell and curse at him when he had answered all my questions. He knew my name. He had even come by the nursery to see me after I was born. He told me that I was the most beautiful baby he had ever seen.

"Please don't shut me out." His crying had slowed a little, but he looked so sad and broken.

It was the ideal time to unleash all my anger and pain on him. He deserved it. He needed to know about the time I was almost raped at the gas station or about the college scholarship I had earned. He needed to hear about how he wasn't at my wedding to give me away or at the birth of his granddaughter. He needed to be punished for missing so much. I had my chance to really drive the point home to him that he was a coward and a loser. Did he care if I missed every father-daughter dance or that I had cried because I had no one to give a Father's Day card to who was really my father? He couldn't understand what it felt like to tell my doctor that I didn't know anything about the health history on my father's side of the family.

The urge to lay it all out before him was tempting. I could make a scene in the restaurant and embarrass him in front of all these people. I could make him regret the day he ever laid eyes on my mom and spawned me. I could finally be the one to turn the tables and hurt him. It didn't matter what he had to say because it wouldn't wipe away 27 years of heartache. It just didn't matter anymore. We were face-to-face now, and I had to make a decision: should I hurt him like he had hurt me or should I let it go?

"Dad?" I looked him in the eyes. I noticed how much we looked alike.

"Please let me explain what happened," he said again.

"You don't have to explain, Dad. It doesn't matter. All that matters is this moment we are in now." I could feel all eyes on us and I started to cry.

"I'm so sorry. Please let me tell you what happened because I know you hate me," he said.

"Dad, I don't hate you. I am happy we found each other and I love you. I want us to start fresh and forget the past. We have both done things that would not make the other proud. Today is a new day that God has given us; let us enjoy it."

With those words, we stood up and hugged. For once, my life felt complete, like it wasn't missing a part. As we hugged, those 27 years passed us by, and all we could do was look forward. Soft clapping erupted around us as the other patrons witnessed a beautiful reunion of father and daughter in a corner booth at the Fish Market in Atlanta in 1999.

Lessons learned

- It's never too late to release the anger over a hurt.

- Every offender has a personal story that mercy leads us to listen to.

- It's only by the grace of God that we desire to move forward in a positive way.

11

Forgiving an Emotionally Unavailable Stepfather

"To forgive is to set a prisoner free and discover the prisoner was you."

UNKNOWN

Trudy was an only child living happily with her mother when this stranger, Mr. Lewis, became a part of their lives. She was excited about the prospect of having a father figure because so many of her friends from the school she attended were from happy two-parent homes. Although her stepfather-to-be didn't speak to her much or even acknowledge her presence, Trudy was sure that once he and her mother were married and they all settled in together, things would change.

Trudy was a bright, affable, and affectionate child. She would often dance, skip around, or play the piano to the delight of her mother. After the much-anticipated wedding, where Trudy was a giggling flower girl, the stepfather found no joy in her attempts to entertain him. To the outside world, the Lewises looked like a happy family. Trudy's last name was even changed to Lewis. But even in her childhood innocence, she recognized that things were beginning to take a downward spiral.

The household rules changed drastically. Mr. Lewis's philosophy was that children were to be seen and not heard. Soon, Trudy was barely seen because the minute her stepfather got home from work, she had to retreat to her room—no dancing around, no playing the piano, and no sitting in the family room. She was gradually being transformed from a happy-go-lucky little girl to a sad and withdrawn only child. Her dreams of gaining a father were dashed when her stepfather told her to call him Mr. Lewis and not Dad. This was almost too much for her little heart to bear.

As the years progressed, the relationship between Trudy and her stepfather became even more distant. When he and her mother divorced a few years later following a string of violent upheavals, Trudy completely despised him. Not only had he hurt her, but he had hurt her mother as well. His voice reverberated often in her head: "You are so clumsy." "Get out of my way." "You are good for nothing but books." She hated him.

She was delighted to rid herself of the surname Lewis when she got married. In her heart, she believed she could more easily forgive a mass murderer than she could this man. She dismissed him from her life vowing not to even regard him as a human being let alone a stepfather. Even though her mother had forgiven him and had urged her to, Trudy could not bring herself to do it.

Over the next several years, life dealt Trudy her fair share of blows. She became a divorce casualty twice and had to raise her four children as a single mom. When her daughter Mattie faced a life-threatening illness, it shook Trudy to her core. She would do anything for the healing of her child.

One day in prayer, she felt an overwhelming sense that she was to forgive her stepfather. Trudy protested, "No, God, not him!" She realized that her faith to believe God for Mattie's healing was severely hampered by her refusal to forgive this man who had hurt her as a child. Eventually, Trudy sought God's help in letting go of the bitterness that stood in the way of her spiritual well-being and Mattie's healing. The pressure was unrelenting. Forgiveness was her only option. It wasn't easy, but as the months went by, God began to do a work in her heart.

At a very low point in her life, her stepfather humbly reentered her life, asking for her forgiveness. He had accepted the Lord, and his newfound faith in Christ was clearly not an act. Mr. Lewis was a new creature. His disposition, speech, and behavior had changed. He had become kind and loving.

Over time, the father-daughter relationship Trudy had longed for as a child came to fruition. They shared many deep conversations. He showed the love and support to her children that she had wished for as a child. He helped her through her financial woes and provided sound counsel.

Forgiveness had paved the way for Trudy to experience the love of an earthly father even in her adult years. With tears in her eyes, Trudy related to me the deep joy she felt the first time she was able to call him Dad and present him with a Father's Day card—such a simple act with a profound effect. Trudy proclaims, "I firmly believe that forgiving my stepfather paved the way for Mattie's healing."

Perhaps this story pales in comparison to your experience with an uncaring, insensitive, abusive, or generally evil stepparent. Whatever the depths of your suffering, God has not left you alone. It's time to step out of your history and step into "His story" for your life.

Lessons learned

You still have an opportunity to positively impact your circle of influence by:

- Refusing to rehearse the wrongs perpetrated against you and disciplining your mind to stay in the present versus opening old wounds.

- Considering that your abuser may have once been a victim of abuse. Resolve not to perpetuate the cycle by becoming an abuser yourself.

- Knowing that trouble is a powerful teacher. Recall the lessons learned from the experience and willingly share them with others—with an overcomer's attitude.

12

Forgiving an Ex-Spouse
Sharing the Blame for the Breakup

All the ways of a man are pure in his own eyes,
but the LORD weighs the spirits.

PROVERBS 16:2

Today in the United States there are more single than married people. One of the contributing causes is divorce. I'd dare say that no couple enters marriage expecting it to end before their death. Unfortunately, divorce is a common reality—even between people of faith.

The betrayal, grief, and resentment that come with the end of a marriage can be hard to overcome. Forgiving an ex-spouse can be a long process, and without forgiveness, many will not be able to free themselves to love again and to move on with their lives. Forgiveness is important especially if children are involved and the couple must learn to co-parent effectively. Angry, fighting parents can cause much anxiety for children. Thus, the willingness to forgive an ex-spouse is vital to a child's emotional well-being.

The dynamics that end a marriage are complicated and often difficult to sort out. It is rarely one person's fault, and self-reflection is important after a divorce. Wise, emotionally mature people often work with a pastor, counselor, or objective friend to determine how they contributed to the divorce and what role the former spouse played in the breakup. Not only is this step critical to define specific actions a person needs to forgive, but it will also help to identify areas where they have fallen short and perhaps should ask for forgiveness from their former spouse and from God.

Terri, a divorcee, enrolled in a drug recovery program and finally realized she needed to ask her ex-husband, Ted, for forgiveness for her part in the failure of their marriage. Her drug use was a major factor that ended the relationship, but his physical, mental, and emotional abuse also played a big role. She knew that even if she apologized for her drug use, there was no way Ted would ever admit his part. She decided to ask his forgiveness anyway to help her stay clean and sober.

Terri had recently moved to a new apartment, and she found some of Ted's books in a box she was unpacking. She used them as an excuse to make an appointment to see him.

"I prayed that I would know what to say," she said. "I dreaded doing this so much that I told myself if I couldn't find a parking place close to his office, I wouldn't go through with it. Providentially, there was a spot right in front of the door."

Several months before, Terri had begun praying for Ted. Her hatred and bitterness were so deep that she could pray only that he would get the punishment he deserved. Over time, she began to change her prayer to ask for God's will for him. She began trying to pray that Ted would receive the abundance of all of God's blessings.

Terri met with Ted that day and told him that she was getting help for her addiction. "I still wasn't sure what I was going to say, but then the perfect thing came out of my mouth: 'I'm sorry things turned out the way they did.' I truly *was* sorry that I'd hurt him and that he'd hurt me. That one little phrase summed it all up without blaming him."

She was right about one thing: Ted did not apologize for his abusive behavior. Notwithstanding, something happened to Terri in that moment. "I realized that I had forgiven him," she said. "I had gone there asking for his forgiveness, and God gave me the ability to forgive him instead—even though he never accepted any responsibility for our divorce."

Terri was motivated to continue her recovery and completely change her life. She and Ted had no children together, so there was no reason for ongoing interactions. However, years later they had a brief encounter at a social function and were able to enjoy a cordial conversation.

"I learned a lot about forgiveness that day when I went to his office," Terri says. "I found that the other person doesn't even have to be repentant for me to bless them and let them go. Ephesians 4:31 became real to me that day: 'Let all bitterness, wrath, anger, clamor, and evil speaking be put away from you, with all malice. And be kind to one another, tenderhearted, for-giving one another, even as God in Christ forgave you.'

"Forgiving someone who isn't repentant frees us. However, as Christians attempting to emulate the life of Christ, we have to model repentance to the world as well as to those who have wronged us, who refuse to accept responsibility for their actions, or even who refuse to change.

"It's easy to respond with anger and vengeful thoughts when a marriage dissolves, but ultimately the person who gets destroyed is the one harboring all those toxic feelings. I was rescued when I repented and asked God to remove my negative thoughts and feelings. This simple act opened the door to my spiritual and emotional growth.

"You'll find as you continue to let go of all the negative emotions surrounding the breakup of your marriage that you become more willing to forgive. Your heart must be open to receive God's grace. If it is full of anger, resentment, bitterness, and rage, you can't receive the gifts of freedom, joy, love, and happiness."

Lessons learned

You can overcome your negative emotions toward your former spouse and begin taking steps to freedom through forgiveness by:

- Acknowledging your part in the divorce, even if your only "fault" was to tolerate or enable the negative behavior.

- Understanding what really happened in the relationship so that you can define what behavior or habits you need to abandon in future relationships.

- Praying for your ex-spouse out of obedience to God and even asking that God would give them an abundance of blessings rather than punishment.

- Making a commitment to forgive your spouse even if they never repent or admit responsibility for their negative behavior.

13

Forgiving a Betraying Wife
Thriving After Adultery

*"He who is without sin among you, let
him throw a stone at her first."*

JOHN 8:7

My husband, Darnell, and I met Bob and Audrey Meisner many
years ago when we were invited to do a segment on marriage
on the *It's a New Day* Canadian television program in Winni-
peg. I was immediately struck by Audrey's infectious laughter
and her fun-loving spirit. Bob's personality seemed to comple-
ment hers perfectly. We enjoyed our fellowship with them and
with Audrey's parents, Willard and Betty Thiessen, founders
and head of the television ministry.

Once, when Bob and Audrey joined us for dinner during a
brief layover in Los Angeles, we spent the entire evening in side-
splitting laughter. Here was a couple who enjoyed each other,
enjoyed their family, and passionately pursued God's purpose
for their lives. They were the picture of an ideal Christian couple. They had three beautiful children, a rewarding career in
sharing the gospel, and the admiration of thousands of viewers.

Bob and Audrey had met and fallen in love in Bible college.
After they were married, they dove right into ministry with its
many pressures. They enjoyed their work, but the stress of it all
sometimes caused tension. Further, their communication tended
to be one-sided when it came to putting their issues on the table.

Bob was comfortable telling Audrey about her shortcomings, but she was intimated by his emotional reaction when she made mistakes or succumbed to other shortcomings. Consequently, Audrey fell into the common but destructive pattern of keeping quiet for peace sake regarding her expectations and desires for their marriage. Further, she decided to become blameless and to perform to the best of her ability to keep Bob from yelling at her.

Their lives started to unravel after 17 years of marriage when Audrey confessed to an adulterous relationship. A few months later, they also learned of her unexpected pregnancy with a biracial child. How could this have happened to such a solid couple? Could their marriage really be restored after this major hit?

I had many questions when I heard the news—as did the thousands of viewers who had watched them host television segments that encouraged strong marriages and upright living. But the seeds of the affair were germinating long before Audrey committed adultery.

> During the first seventeen years of my marriage, the pattern of my sexual thoughts seemed innocent to me. I wouldn't have admitted a problem about them even to my very best friend because I never recognized it as a problem myself. Bob was totally unaware. I routinely fantasized scenarios that made our lovemaking "forbidden" and it added excitement for me. In my mind, I always justified it with the excuse, "At least I'm with my husband." My thoughts were closely associated with my actions...
>
> A man entered our lives whom Bob and I were trying to help. He took an immediate interest in me,

lavishing me with praise and attention and expressions of appreciation whenever he could. I wasn't emotionally ready for such a continual barrage of affection and affirmation, even though I thought I was.[5]

Before long, their relationship became sexual. When Audrey confessed her sin, naturally Bob was furious. In recounting the experience during a television interview on the *700 Club*, Bob admits, "I wanted to punch holes in the walls, slam doors, express anger and rage!"[6] Instead, he reached out to a marriage counselor in Phoenix, Arizona, who had been a guest on their TV show. He and Audrey flew there the next day. The counselor got to the core of their problem and ministered life-changing principles from the Word of God that helped them get on the road to restoration. He emphasized to Bob the importance of stepping into the role of "covering" his wife and family. Bob explains:

> This understanding didn't happen instantly on our first night with Leo [the counselor] at all. I wanted to be angry. I deserved to be angry...It was my lack of understanding of the covering principle that caused me at first to want to tell everybody what Audrey had done and to declare my innocence, making her the villain and me the hero...Leo had recognized that danger right away and immediately cut it off, reminding me of Proverbs 25:2 that says, "It is the glory of God to conceal a matter." God's desire for our situation was healing and restoration, which called for, first of all, concealing or covering it for protection. Every woman has a deep down desire to be covered; it is part of her God-designed

makeup. Every man is designed by God to be a cov-
erer, a protector of his wife and children.[7]

Bob and Audrey resigned their pastoral and TV hosting
positions in Canada and relocated to Phoenix to start a new life.
Five months later, the baby was born.

Bob exudes, "This little boy was nothing but a gift, an abso-
lute gift. When our son was born, I gave him my name, Robert,
middle name Theodore and then Meisner because I don't want
my son to ever question one day in his life whose boy he is. Theodore means 'divine gift.'"[8]

Bob and Audrey's marriage is stronger today and their communication is open and direct. Yes, they lost a few supporters,
people who just refused to forgive. However, they are finding
great joy in taking their message of forgiveness and hope to cou-
ples around the world through their books, conference presen-
tations, and television show *MyNewDay.tv*. I was surprised but
delighted when they made the courageous decision to chron-
icle their story of restoration in a groundbreaking book, *Marriage Under Cover: Thriving in a Culture of Quiet Desperation*.

Lessons learned

- No mistake or tragedy can thwart God's ultimate
  purpose for our lives (Isaiah 14:27). Like a GPS,
  when we make a wrong turn, our heavenly Father
  who sees all and knows all just "recalculates" a different route to our Divine destiny.

- God not only forgives but also redeems, restores,
  and releases a willing vessel back into service in His
  kingdom for His glory.

14

Forgiving an Irresponsible Brother
Abandoning Judgment

*So the LORD said to Cain, "Why are you angry? And why
has your countenance fallen? If you do well, will you not
be accepted? And if you do not do well, sin lies at the door.
And its desire is for you, but you should rule over it."*

GENESIS 4:6-7

Sibling rivalry has been an issue in families since the beginning of time. Cain, Adam and Eve's firstborn, killed his brother,
Abel, because God accepted Abel's sacrifice but rejected Cain's
offering. Of course, we are all familiar with the story of Joseph
and how his brothers, because of envy that he was their father's
favorite child, sold him into slavery at the tender age of 17.

Today, brothers and sisters still fight and carry resentments.
Some are jealous of another's God-given gifts or the attention
they get from the parents. In the final analysis, sibling rivalry
is about establishing personal worth and value. Siblings com-
pete and compare talents, skills, and abilities to see who "wins."
Sometimes Mom and Dad unwittingly instigate the competition by challenging a son or daughter to "be like your brother
(or sister)" or by simply aligning themselves with the child
whose personality is most like their own. They continue in this
destructive path when their children become adults by appear-
ing to be more proud of the one with the most possessions or
the best performance in the arenas of life.

Parents could minimize sibling rivalry by celebrating each child's uniqueness and emphasizing their equal value in God's sight. Notwithstanding, for most siblings, the strife and competition usually give way to forgiveness and harmony.

Pete's story is a little different. Pete is two years older than his brother, Mark. When they were young, Pete was the athlete, the straight-A student who seemed to succeed at everything he did. Mark, challenged with learning disabilities, was a mediocre student and had no athletic ability. Their father spent more time with Pete because they shared the same interests of hunting, fishing, and football.

When Pete graduated from high school, he couldn't wait to be independent. He went to college in another state and began a successful career as an auditor in a major city within three hours of his parents' home. Mark, who went to college locally, never moved out of the house. Pete got married and had two children. Mark had a job but made no plans to move out of his parents' home. Pete started having financial problems because of a layoff at work and was resentful that his brother was living rent-free and could afford the nice car and other things that Pete could not.

Pete's resentment grew over the years to the point that he couldn't stand to be around his brother. Pete and his family visited his parents only on major holidays, and he had as little to do with his brother as possible. His wife complained that all Pete ever talked about was how angry he was at Mark. Then one day Pete's dad called, asking him to join him on a hunting trip. Pete went, and while they were sitting around the campfire, his father told him he had stage-four lung cancer.

"I was blindsided," Pete said. "Then I thought of all the birthdays and anniversaries and other family events I had skipped because I hated Mark. I was punishing my parents because I was angry at my brother."

For the first time, Pete poured out his feelings about Mark to his father. He quietly listened to Pete's story, and then he smiled. "You realize that Mark has always been envious of you, don't you?" his father said. "You were the basketball hero, the honor roll student, and the guy who always dated the cute girls. Mark thought everything came easy for you while he had to work himself to death just to be average."

Pete then realized that his brother's only way of feeling good about himself was to have things that he knew Pete couldn't afford. "Mark wasn't married nor did he have many friends," Pete said. "Possessions were the only thing he had that he felt could put him on my level. He felt like he was on top for a change."

Driving home from the hunting trip, Pete had another realization. "It suddenly dawned on me that it was none of my business if my brother was living rent-free in my parents' house. That's between them and Mark. I certainly didn't want to spend my life in my parents' basement, but if he does, that's his prerogative."

A month later, Pete went to visit his parents to talk about his father's treatment and care. "Mark volunteered to use his vacation time to take Dad to chemo and radiation and to stay home a day or two a week to give Mom time to rest from taking care of Dad," Pete said. "At first I got angry, thinking it was just his way of becoming more dependent on my parents. But then I realized they needed him. I had a family I needed to support financially and emotionally, and Mark taking care of our parents was lifting a huge burden off me."

Pete began adding his brother to his prayers when he and his wife did their morning devotional together. He noticed when he went to visit his dad now he wasn't as resentful toward Mark. "It wasn't about us anymore," Pete said. "It was about Dad and Mom."

Despite treatment, Pete's father's health continued to decline. One winter afternoon, both of the brothers sat at their father's bedside as he lay dying. He opened his eyes and smiled.

"I've always been so proud of both of you," Pete's father said. "But I've never been more proud of you as I am now. I can go to my Maker now knowing that you'll both be here for your mother. That makes me so happy."

Pete's father took his last breath an hour later.

"After the funeral home came and Mom went to bed, I asked Mark if he wanted a beer," Pete said. "We went out on the porch and talked about all those stories that only your sibling knows— like that summer Dad grounded me for staying out all night or the time the Christmas tree fell over because Dad didn't set it up right. We laughed and we cried. After that, things were different between Mark and me."

Pete and Mark never apologized to each other, but Pete realized that he had hurt his brother as much as his brother had hurt him. Praying for Mark prepared Pete's heart to forgive his brother and reconcile at a time in their lives when they desperately needed each other.

Lessons learned

- It's important to ask God to give you the willingness to forgive all perceived and real offenses.

- Ask a neutral third party to help you determine if you contributed something to the situation.

- Be sensitive to the discomfort you create for everyone who is affected by the fractured relationship between you and your sibling.

- Be the proactive peacemaker; make the first move toward reconciliation.

15

Forgiving an Evil Sister
From Abuse to Adoration

Be kind to one another, tenderhearted, forgiving
one another, even as God in Christ forgave you.

EPHESIANS 4:32

Yolanda's Story

"Shut up, Stupid!" The words stung. But not as much as the
flurry of hard slaps to my five-year-old face. It was not the first
time my sister Martina would assault me nor would it be the last.
Three years older than I, Marty seemed to revel in the name-
calling, hair-pulling, scratch-inflicting episodes that would be
repeated until I was eleven years old. These attacks were beyond
the innocuous tussle that sometime happens between siblings
over toys and such. These were brutal beatings administered
with a rage that belied my sister's youth and left me in abject
terror.

The only saving grace was that we didn't reside in the same
household. I lived full-time with my godmother in an upper
middle-class neighborhood across town, while Marty and three
of my other sisters lived with our biological mother in an impov-
erished section of South Central Los Angeles. Our father's drug
addiction and Mama's ill health had made it necessary for her
to place some of us in the homes of friends. Eventually, most

of my siblings came back home to live. I did not. Compared to my sisters, I lived in a paradise. My godmother and I lived in a stylishly decorated two-bedroom duplex, while my mother and sisters subsisted in a vermin-infested, converted garage. I admit I dreaded visits to my mother's house. My sisters were virtual strangers with whom I had to share a bed. Back home I had my own room complete with every amenity—including a television set. It was quite a luxury for an African-American child growing up in the 1960s.

I'm sure that my expensive clothing and childish air of entitlement did little to endear me to my sister's heart. She resented me for my advantages and she demonstrated that resentment often. Whenever I'd visit, whether it was for a weekend or an entire summer, Marty would take every opportunity to get me alone to exact her punishment. Each time, a threat of future beatings would keep me from telling anyone. Bruises and scratches were convincingly explained away.

Oddly enough, I don't recall ever thinking of ways to retaliate. Fact is, I was in awe of my sister. I thought (and still think) she is one of the smartest and most beautiful people I know. I admired her fashion sense and how her jet-black afro hairstyle was always perfect. Our mother doted on Marty because of the potential she saw in her. She even managed to save money from her meager earnings to enroll my sister in modeling school. In her eyes, Marty was a star.

At 14, Marty became pregnant. When Mama found out, she beat her severely. Our mother's high hopes for my sister were crushed and she took her frustration out on Marty's back.

Shortly after Marty gave birth to her son, I came to visit.

Her hair was no longer perfectly coiffed and she appeared older somehow. It seems nothing had prepared her for the responsibilities of caring for a newborn. Late-night feedings, diaper changes, and colic were now her world. Mama had been adamant that Marty continue to attend school each day. My sister was simply worn out. There had been no violent episodes between us during her pregnancy, so I felt safe for a change. That sense of security was short-lived.

One evening while Mama was out, I committed some small infraction (I can't even remember what it was), but it sent my sister into a rage. However, this night would mark the last time she would ever touch me. As Marty moved toward me with arm raised and her hand prepared to strike, I took a step backward, squared my shoulders, and declared in the most menacing voice I could muster, "If you hit me, I will kill your baby." My words stopped her in her tracks.

"What?" she said, her hand still raised. "What did you say?"

"You won't know when and you won't know how, but I will kill him," I continued, feeling brave for the first time in my life—even though I had no intention of carrying out my evil threat.

What happened next proved to be the catalyst for a miracle of forgiveness and healing. Marty, my lifelong antagonist, the source of my every childhood fear, slowly withdrew her hand, sank to the floor, and sobbed. I was taken aback. I'd never seen her be vulnerable before—ever. Even though I was too young to be able to articulate what I was feeling, I had compassion for her. The one who seemed so invincible was suddenly destructible. I was sorry that I had hurt her and told her so.

From that moment on, I no longer saw my sister as some ferocious beast but as a wounded and broken human being. The ensuing years would reveal that my sister hurt me because she had been so terribly hurt by others. Today, we are in our fifties. Marty is the person I'm the closest to in the world. She is beyond my sister—she is my best friend. Our relationship is one of loving acceptance. More than restored, the relationship was renewed. That is the power of forgiveness.

I can truly say there is no residual pain of the hurt in my heart. I hardly ever think of those days. And, if there is any hurt at all, it is the pain of seeing the fleeting regret that sometimes passes through my sister's eyes. I know that she hasn't completely forgiven herself. I pray that someday she will be able to experience the liberating peace that comes when you let someone go—even if that someone is yourself.

I believe that the ability to forgive my own flesh and blood for such atrocious acts has given me an uncommon ability to forgive others. When my husband decided he wanted out of our marriage, it was that same miracle of forgiveness that allowed us to become supportive friends again after several years of hurt feelings.

Because God has forgiven us for our sins, who are we not to forgive others? Unconditional forgiveness is not a natural ability. It is a Divine character attribute that develops only as we grow closer to God. To be in Christ is to do as Christ does—"Father, forgive them for they know not what they do." And that is the miracle.

Lessons learned

- True forgiveness is total and complete.

- True forgiveness holds no one's heart for ransom.

- The grace of God helps us not to carry an offense. While my sister did eventually ask me to forgive her, it was not a requirement because the work had already been done. She knew by my words and actions that I held no offense.

16

Forgiving a Friend—Without Restoring the Relationship

Even my best friend, the one I trusted completely,
the one who shared my food, has turned against me.

PSALM 41:9 NLT

Sabrina and Vonda were inseparable. They had been friends since kindergarten and continued to be close through high school. Sabrina had a boyfriend, Mel, who became friends with Vonda as well.

Vonda's eighteenth birthday was approaching, and Sabrina and Mel planned a night of dinner, mini-golf, and a late-night walk on the beach for her. But when the big day approached, Sabrina was sick.

"She told me to go ahead and celebrate my birthday with Mel," Vonda said. "I told her I felt uncomfortable doing it, but Sabrina insisted."

Vonda and Mel had a lot of fun. They both enjoyed each other's company, and Mel told Vonda, in a joking way, he liked hanging out with her better than Sabrina. Then he kissed her.

"I was caught up in the moment," Vonda said. "I kissed him back. I felt guilty immediately."

After a week or so, Vonda told Sabrina about the kiss and begged her for forgiveness. Sabrina said that she had wanted to break up with Mel anyway, and it was no big deal.

"I was so relieved," Vonda said. "I thought it was all behind us. Then a girl I didn't even know approached me at school and called me a whore for having sex with my best friend's boyfriend. She told me Sabrina had told her that. Pretty soon it was all over the school."

Vonda was furious. "I was angry because Sabrina had told me that we were okay. And not only that, I had lost my best friend during the senior year that we had been looking forward to."

Sabrina and Vonda's mutual friends begged them to call a truce. "We didn't. In fact, it got worse," Vonda said. "For the next eight years we refused to be in the same room with each other. It caused so much pain for our friends because they were either forced to choose between us or just not invite either of us to any of their baby showers, weddings, or other get-togethers."

"I would lay awake at night thinking of ways to get back at Sabrina," Vonda said. "I couldn't think of anything good enough to create the kind of pain I felt. My hate consumed me and turned me into a person I didn't want to be."

Vonda left town to go to college and kept in touch with some of her high school friends. After a time she began making new friends, but she didn't trust them. She kept relationships superficial and missed the deep connection she had had with Sabrina. "The loneliness forced me to look to God for my comfort," Vonda said. "I had never had a relationship with Him before, but now I really needed to have that connection. That was the grace that came out of this situation."

Sabrina did finally break up with Mel and began dating another guy. They married soon after. "Sabrina wanted to be a lawyer," Vonda said. "She dropped out of college to marry this guy, and that would have never happened if I had been in her life. I felt bad for her. Then her mother died suddenly and Sabrina had to raise her two younger sisters. I wouldn't wish that on anyone."

After Vonda graduated from college and had begun a successful career, she went home for another old friend's wedding. "I knew Sabrina would be there, but by now I didn't care. I decided that I could be the bigger person."

Vonda approached Sabrina, and the two old friends chatted for a while. "She looked so defeated and sad," Vonda said. "Her marriage wasn't working out, but she didn't make enough money on her own to support her and her sisters. She was trapped."

Sabrina confessed to Vonda that she hadn't been sick the night of Vonda's birthday. "It was a setup so that she could break up with Mel, just as I had suspected," Vonda said. "She was very sorry for everything that she had done."

At that point, Vonda forgave Sabrina. "I realized that she wasn't a strong person and I felt pity for her," Vonda said. "She didn't have the courage to break up with Mel. She didn't have the courage to continue her education, and she didn't have the courage to leave her abusive husband. She had no one, and she didn't even have God."

Vonda and Sabrina were never good friends again. "Too much had happened, and we were both in very different worlds," Vonda said. "We tried to rekindle the friendship, but we didn't have much in common anymore. I learned during all of this that it was okay to let go of friendships that had run their course."

Sabrina is still on Vonda's prayer list. "She's still married to that abusive guy 15 years later," Vonda said. "I have learned to let that go. I can't fix her, and looking back I think that was the role I had in our friendship."

When a friend betrays us it's often hard to repair the relationship. The lack of trust we experience makes it difficult to trust other friends or let new friends into our lives.

Today Vonda has close friends—even closer than she ever was with Sabrina. "Most of my friends are people of faith who have integrity and aren't afraid to tell me the truth," Vonda said. "I'm truly blessed."

Lessons learned

You can forgive your friends and forge stronger relationships by:

- Putting your relationship with God first
- Praying for your friends
- Learning to let things go that you can't change

17

Forgiving an Insensitive Pastor
Dismantling the Pedestal

*Obey your spiritual leaders, and do what they say. Their work
is to watch over your souls, and they are accountable to God.*

HEBREWS 13:17 NLT

We like to think of church as a safe haven where we can recharge,
serve others, and live in harmony with each other—at least that
idea is a wonderful goal to attempt to attain. But even from the
beginning, the church has experienced strife and hard feelings.
We're all human, after all.

One of the hardest people for many to forgive is their pastor. We tend to believe our church leaders are called by God to a
higher standard of conduct, to serve as a model of living as one
of Jesus's disciples. We forget that pastors are human too. They
make mistakes, and then we make the mistake of believing that
they should be perfect in every aspect.

Letty was one of those people who found it hard to forgive
her pastor. Brother Doug had led the congregation for 15 years.
Letty thought he did a great job preaching, teaching Bible studies, and conducting funerals. Brother Doug had even visited
her mother in the hospital, even though she wasn't a member
of the church.

In recent years, the congregation had started to dwindle.
Fewer young people were coming to the services, and the regular

attenders were concerned that before long there wouldn't be enough money to keep the doors open. The church leaders called a congregational meeting to discuss what to do.

"Almost the entire congregation was there," Letty said. "I felt hopeful that Brother Doug would have the answers."

At first, the meeting was congenial. The Holy Spirit was present, giving members ideas to hold special services and to launch new programming. The excitement in the room was growing as they came up with more ideas to help attract people to the church.

Brother Doug had written about 20 excellent ideas on a whiteboard. Then he stopped the discussion by asking, "So who is going to volunteer to do all of these things?"

"You could hear crickets chirping it got so quiet," Letty said. "I thought about raising my hand and volunteering to help, but I was already teaching Sunday school and involved in our food pantry ministry. I thought that other people should step up."

The room continued to be silent. Pastor Doug laughed nervously. "We can't launch twenty new initiatives without people willing to work on them," he said.

Mavis, an older woman, spoke up. "I'm not teaching children. I did that when I was young and I'm done with that."

Jasper, a middle-age member nodded his head. "Yeah, pastor. I'm in charge of the church grounds and I teach Sunday school too. I can't do anything else."

Oscar, who had a reputation as a troublemaker, stood up at the back of the sanctuary. Everyone turned around in their pews to listen to him. "Isn't that what we pay you for, Brother?"

Brother Doug's face turned red and he started shouting. "I work sixty hours a week on average! I haven't had a vacation in two years! And believe me, Oscar, your five-dollar-a-month tithe barely buys me a cup of coffee!"

Brother Doug stormed out of the sanctuary with Oscar trailing behind, hurling insults at him. Letty was appalled. "I couldn't believe my pastor acted like that," she said. "I knew Oscar was in the wrong, but Brother Doug should have acted better than that."

Pastor Doug took a three-month leave of absence. When he returned he looked happier and healthier than he had in a long time. But Letty couldn't get the image of Pastor Doug's angry face out of her mind. She couldn't forget that he had publicly revealed the amount of Oscar's tithe. She quit going to church for a few weeks, and even visited a few other churches to see if she could find a new church home. Against her better judgment, she decided to return to her old church.

One day, Letty ran into Elva, the church secretary, at the grocery store. They chatted for a minute, and then Elva told Letty that her job was so much better since Brother Doug had returned.

"Doug doesn't reveal a lot about his personal life, but I found out six months ago that his mother was diagnosed with terminal cancer," Elva said. "Then his best friend in seminary got killed in a car wreck. After that his younger brother got shipped out to Afghanistan. Poor guy. I would have lost it too. But now that he's rested, he's back to his old self."

"I would have prayed for him if I had known," Letty told Elva.

"We always need to pray for our pastor no matter what," Elva said. "It's hard to live up there on a pedestal."

"I had no idea," Letty said. "I never had thought about how hard it must be to try to be perfect all the time. With that perspective, I had no trouble forgiving Brother Doug. In fact, I admire how he came back after his leave of absence and took right back up where he left off."

Oscar left the church, and members who had been at odds with him came back. The church began to flourish again. Letty and several others volunteered to be in charge of the 20 initiatives the Holy Spirit gave the congregation during the meeting. Ten years later, when Pastor Doug retired, Letty proudly organized his going-away party.

Lessons learned

- It's important to pray for your pastor every day, knowing that he is human and subject to the same temptations as everyone else.

- Keep him off the pedestal and his position of authority in perspective.

18

Forgiving a Credit-Snatching Boss

For promotion cometh neither from the east,
nor from the west, nor from the south.
But God is the judge: he putteth down
one, and setteth up another.

Psalm 75:6-7 kjv

Most of us spend the majority of our time at work, and when trouble starts at our home away from home, it can create pure misery. No one is productive in an environment where workers resent each other. Forgiving your boss or coworkers is necessary to create a work environment where you can thrive and reach your professional potential.

Amber was a graphic designer at an ad agency. She had won numerous awards for her work and reveled in the creative challenges she faced every day. A new art director, Miles, replaced Amber's old boss, whom she loved. Amber and her coworkers began to notice that Miles had trouble with technology and didn't seem to know how to do any graphic design at all. Although she found this troubling, Amber continued to do her job well and worked with Miles as best she could.

One day, Jarrod popped into Amber's cubicle and asked if she had read Miles's latest email. "You won't believe it," he said. "This guy is a liar and a thief."

Amber immediately opened the email. Miles had inadvertently sent it to all the staff instead of just to his boss. In the email, he attached a report that outlined everything he had done the month previous. Amber was shocked to see that several of her ideas and projects were listed as Miles's accomplishments. In fact, Miles had performed few of the items on the list.

The six graphic artists in Amber's department discussed what to do. There was a lot of complaining and general negativity. Doreen decided she was going to do as little work as possible in protest. Several others decided to do the same thing. Amber did less work for a couple of days, but then she felt guilty about cheating her company out of the time and went back to her regular routine.

A month later, the president of the ad agency called a meeting. She said that the company had lost a key account and that they were laying off a number of people. Half of Amber's department was let go. Amber was spared, but so was Miles.

Amber was convinced that the reports Miles was writing to his boss played a part in determining who was laid off. She grew resentful and didn't enjoy her work anymore. She didn't feel that creative spark she used to have and hated going to work in the morning.

One night a strong thunderstorm woke up Amber's four-year-old son, Owen. He called out to his mother in the middle of the night, terrified. She lay down with him for a few minutes to lull him back to sleep.

"I'm scared, Mommy," he said. "I prayed to God about it, but God didn't stop the storm."

"God is here with us even though the storm hasn't stopped," Amber told him. "He sent me to take care of you."

The next morning as Amber got ready for work, she reflected on what Owen had told her about praying for God to stop the thunderstorm.

"I realized that my prayers had been similar," she said. "I had been praying for God to get Miles to quit or get fired. I recognized that God had the power to do just that, but He had chosen not to. I realized that, just like me being there for Owen during the storm, there were people there for me, supporting me through this tough situation."

Amber changed her prayer to focus on asking for God's will for her life. "I realized that God would give me what I needed in order to work with Miles, and if God didn't, then it was time to move on."

Over the next few weeks, Amber began to not dread work so much. She began engaging in her job again and started feeling her creativity return.

"I know that everyone always says that forgiveness is a choice," she said. "But in this case, I hadn't even considered forgiving Miles. I just decided that I would stop focusing on my resentment and focus on God's presence instead. The byproduct of changing my focus was forgiveness."

Christmas was near when Amber came into the office one morning and saw an envelope on her desk. It contained a bonus check and a note. "The note was from the president and thanked me for doing an exceptional job," she said. "Then he said he'd really liked the brochure I had designed for our local hospital."

Later in the morning, Amber noted that the brochure was one of the projects Miles had taken credit for. "I realized the powers that be had somehow learned that Miles was taking credit for others' work. The acknowledgment from the president meant everything to me."

Amber worked with Miles for two years more, and then he left the company. Amber was pleased to be promoted to his position. "Once I learned that Miles needed to look good; I was able to provide some of that support for him," Amber said. "I was free to do the job I loved, and I didn't worry any more about it. God was always there."

Lessons learned

You can start on the path to forgiving your boss and coworkers by:

- Becoming aware of your resentment and how it's affecting your life

- Making a decision to focus on the positive instead of the negative

- Not participating in feeding your resentment with other coworkers

- Praying for God's will for you every morning and attempting to do what you believe God is calling you to do that day

19

Forgiving a Husband's Killer
A Miscarriage of Justice

*"Never forget the three powerful resources you always
have available to you: love, prayer, and forgiveness."*

H. Jackson Brown Jr.

Adrianna's Story

As the homicide detective stood in front of me describing the
details of what happened the night before, all I could do was sob.

My husband, Jim, had gotten off work and was traveling
home on his motorcycle when a car pulled out in front of him.
He had no time to stop; he smashed into the car. The driver of
the car pulled into a parking lot, and the occupants got out and
walked over to the road where Jim's body lay, broken and bleed-
ing. Then, they got back in their car and drove away.

They hid out behind a trailer a few miles from where the accident occurred. They were later caught and arrested after a tip
from a witness. They were all drunk, and all living and working
illegally in the United States. Within hours, they were bailed out
of jail and running free. They would never be seen again and
never brought to trial in Alabama for their crime.

For a year after Jim's death, I carried so much hatred for His-
panics. I could not stand the sight of them. I wanted them all to
leave and go back to Mexico. This was not like me. I had never

been a prejudiced person. Then again, I had never had to tell my daughter that her daddy had died and watch her go through so much pain. I had never had to experience so much grief in my life. Hate is a strong emotion, and I was feeling it every day toward an entire group of people because of the acts of just a few.

A year after the accident I had thrown myself into a new project to take my mind off things. My Sunday school class had started a food pantry. My days became filled with collecting canned goods and other nonperishables. My weekends were spent at the church counting food or painting and hanging shelves. Although I was doing a good and charitable act, my heart was still hard like concrete.

One day, as I counted the last of the day's donations, I realized we would be able to help many families in our community with the food we had collected. I made an announcement to our congregation and handed out flyers about the food available at the pantry.

About a week later, I received an email from a teacher at a local elementary school. The subject line read, "Family in Need." She started by explaining that she had found my flyer and knew a family that could use our help. She didn't go to my church and she did not know me. She went on to explain that the family consisted of a single mother and young children. I read the email over and over and began to cry. I looked up and screamed out to God, "Why?" The family this teacher was describing was the family of the man driving the car that caused the accident that resulted in my husband's death.

I resisted the temptation to delete the message. I knew that if I did, I would be the only one to know besides God, and I would have to answer to Him. I was so angry that God had allowed me to go through so much pain and now He wanted me to help this family!

For an hour, I wrestled with God about what to do, and I finally broke down. I thought about this woman and how she may never see her husband again. I thought about her children and how they may never see their father again. I thought about their struggles and their pain. I realized we were a lot alike. I also realized that day that the man driving the car didn't purposely kill my husband and that his entire race was not to blame.

With my face to the floor and my tears flowing, I forgave this man. I pleaded with the Lord to forgive me for all the hatred and resentment I had been carrying around for so long.

The next weekend, I carried the box of food up the tiny steps of their trailer. I met the mother and her four beautiful children. It was bittersweet but truly a blessing. I did not mention that we had a common connection. She will never know how it came to be that the wife of the man her husband killed was sitting in her living room with a box of food. She will never know how much I wanted to tell her, but instead prayed with her and over her family. My heart was bursting, and it took all I had not to break down in her home that day. God gave me the strength to face her and to love her as though she were my neighbor. It did not matter that day that she was Hispanic or poor. It did not matter that she couldn't speak English or that I couldn't speak Spanish. All that mattered was that God had forgiven me and I had forgiven her husband. In that moment, I felt great joy.

Because of that day when I got that email, I am now able to look back on the past few years since the accident and see God at work in my life and the life of my daughter. I think back on that homicide detective talking to me and realize how difficult his job had been. I pray for the man that caused the accident and hope that he is saved.

Lessons learned

- God is perfect in all that he does, and sometimes it takes us getting down to the very darkest places in our hearts to see what He wants us to do.

- He allowed me to make a decision that would affect not only my life here on earth but also my eternal life in heaven.

- His timing is perfect and often takes us by surprise. He took the weight of all that resentment I had been carrying around and lifted it from me. He made me face what I didn't want to face—and to seek Him to deal with it.

20

Forgiving a Molester
Surviving by the Grace of God

*See to it that no one fails to obtain the grace of
God; that no "root of bitterness" springs up and
causes trouble, and by it many become defiled.*

Hebrews 12:15 esv

Diana's Story

My mom and dad divorced when I was 12 years old. A short
time later, Mom married a sailor named Wally. My sister Mary
and I moved with them to military housing on the base. My
three older siblings had already left home.

Both Mom and Wally were extremely sociable. They threw
many weekend parties when Wally was not on duty. They were
heavy drinkers, and my mom would often drink until she
passed out. After their guests would leave, Wally would come
into my room and make inappropriate advances toward me.
He was very stealthy and made sure that my younger sister was
sound asleep in the twin bed next to mine. I was shocked and
embarrassed by his intrusion. I would hiss, "Take your hands off
of me!" But each weekend—or whenever he drank too much—
he would make his dreaded visit.

I threatened to tell Mom, but that did not frighten him at
all. He continued to touch me in inappropriate places. Whenever I had to miss a day from school because of illness or other

reasons, he would leave the naval base, come home, and make a beeline to my bedroom to continue his degrading acts.

What could I do? Wally warned that if I told anyone about his behavior, he would kill me and my entire family. I contemplated suicide. I also considered telling his navy commander about his behavior.

I did everything I could to avoid encounters with Wally. I would arise very early each weekday morning, quickly dress, and run to the school bus stop long before its scheduled departure time. I would be the only one there. Many times I would be cold and hungry, but I had to get out of that house before he woke up and began his fondling routine.

I prayed my mother would catch him, but his timing seemed impeccable. I finally mustered the courage to tell her. To my dismay, she didn't believe me. In fact, she'd begun showing animosity toward me from the time my biological father had left home when he discovered her infidelity; now it intensified and the beatings started. Wally would accuse me of breaking dishes, eating forbidden foods, and any other acts that would raise my mother's ire. She would beat me unmercifully even though I denied his accusations.

"Are you calling me a liar?" he would yell. Asserting my innocence only motivated him to take his turn beating me. An extension cord was their favorite disciplining tool, and boy, did it leave its mark! Some of the scars are still visible today.

My body was riddled with welts; blood often poured from my back. I wanted to report the beatings to the school, but I was afraid and ashamed. Mom and Wally threatened that I'd better not say anything to anyone. I couldn't take gym classes because a few times my teacher had spotted bruises on me and wanted to know how they got there. I lied because I was afraid of the consequences I'd suffer at home.

Mom and Wally also verbally abused me, calling me every name in the book. Their neglect was unimaginable. They would not give me any lunch money, and I often had no dinner. Hunger pains were my constant companion. I went to school with holes in my shoes. Sometimes it was just too much to bear. I would cry myself to sleep every night.

I was failing in school and no longer wanted to go back. The teachers complained about my grades. My report card was horrible. The abuse had been horrific, and my whole nervous system seemed to be torn to pieces. The depression was overwhelming. I feared practically everything, and my self-esteem hit rock bottom.

I ended up meeting a boy and getting pregnant when I was 15. My mother promptly put me out of the house. The baby's father denied responsibility, forcing me to seek financial relief from the county social services department. I was devastated at being pregnant, but I was just happy to get out of the house. Though I was very young, I was able to get a studio apartment and began a new life, meeting different people and making new friends. I later moved to another city with my Aunt Sara. Wally and my mother finally parted ways.

Through much prayer and pastoral counseling, as well as mentoring from the seasoned older ladies of the church, I learned that I was not to blame for Wally's actions. I found peace within. I stood on the truth that I was the innocent one and he the guilty one. The pain that I suffered at his hand still affects me when I hear of others that face the same abuse.

I saw Wally only a couple of times after I relocated. I had held so much unforgiveness and hatred inside that I felt I needed to forgive him in order to move in a positive direction with my life. It took over 30 years, but by the grace of God, I finally forgave him. He could have made it easier if he'd just admitted what he'd done and apologized for stealing my childhood. Years later, I confronted him about it, and he showed no sign of remorse. "You wanted it as much as I did," he said. Nothing could have been further from the truth. Sometime later, I heard that he died on the floor of his apartment all alone.

I did not find out until many years later that Wally had also been molesting Mary. Oh, how that broke my heart. I had promised her that I would come back for her. Being practically a child myself at the time, I didn't keep my promise. I sensed strong resentment and emotional distance from my dear sister over the years. She finally confessed that she had unforgiveness in her heart toward me because I hadn't rescued her. It never occurred to me that she too might become Wally's victim. We eventually talked through and healed our relationship. I'm so happy that we did because six years after admitting her hurt and unforgiveness, she passed away.

If only I could warn every child not to be afraid to tell a teacher, parent, or other responsible adult if someone is doing something to them that is not appropriate—even if the perpetrator threatens to kill their loved ones. Odds are they won't. It is best to get help, even when afraid. I only wish I had used that common sense and not let fear prevail. I also wish I'd not let unforgiveness take away the many years I could have been fruitful.

Rarely these days do I think of the shame and abuse Wally perpetrated against me. I have truly forgiven him. Before my mom died, I also forgave her for not protecting me and my sister. I had not spoken to her for nearly 15 years, but before she took her last breath, I was there to say goodbye to her. I hope my story helps other hurting folks, especially children.

Diana was able to move forward with her life. She vowed never to repeat the bad parenting she was subjected to. She kept her word. She is the loving mother of eight children. She is also a highly regarded counselor and Bible teacher who prays for the healing and deliverance of other hurting people of all ages and walks of life.

Lessons learned

- Fear will threaten an unlikely outcome to bully you into not taking wise actions.

- A brother or sister is born to help in time of need (Proverbs 17:17), so it's important to reach out for support to the people God has put in your life.

- You are not bound to repeat the sins of your parents if you submit them to God.

21

Forgiving a Rapist
Justice Served

For the LORD loves justice,
and he will never abandon the godly.

PSALM 37:28 NLT

Annie's Story

I was raped by the pastor of my church for over three consecutive months. I was thirteen years old. My drug-addicted mom and I lived around the corner from the church. Pastor Harry had agreed with my mom to take me to school each day. The abuse began immediately. He would rape me and then verbally abuse me afterward, calling me a dirty whore and other degrading names. He threatened to kill me if I told anyone about his actions. He also threatened to rape my nieces, who were five and seven years old at the time. I was in constant fear that he would hurt or kill me.

When I became pregnant by him at age fourteen, my fears grew worse. I felt I would be better off telling my godmother, who was also my mom's drug counselor. She was livid! She reported it to the police and Pastor Harry was arrested. We prayed that others would come forward, and they did—six of them. I aborted the baby I was carrying.

Pastor Harry was charged with five counts of child molestation and rape and six counts of taking kids across the state line with sexual intent. Television and other media carried the story. His small congregation remained fiercely loyal to him and sent hate mail and threats to my house. I escaped further harassment by relocating to another state. I returned to the city two years later to testify at his trial. He is currently serving a 30-year sentence in a state prison.

I am now 17. Only in the past year have I forgiven myself and let go of the guilt of having an abortion. I am still healing from all the trauma of this ordeal; it's a daily process. I sometimes experience sadness when thinking about the child I aborted and the disappointment of knowing I cannot give my future husband my virginity.

Fortunately, God dealt with me about forgiving Pastor Harry. Initially, I had no desire to forgive him, but my mentor explained that forgiveness was not for his benefit but mine. I needed to be free of the emotional bondage so I could live out God's purpose for my life. I opened my heart to the Spirit's wooing. My faith played a big role in my decision to forgive. Thank God for a solid church and a godly pastor who teaches the importance of forgiving. God healed my emotions. I wrote Pastor Harry a letter telling him that I'd forgiven him and was praying he would experience God's grace and mercy.

I have learned that you are not responsible for what others do to you. What happens to you does not have to define you; God defines you at creation for His Divine purpose. I also learned that God is a God of restoration, healing, and new beginnings.

Even though Satan tried to destroy me, God had the final say—and He says I am victorious. I am currently completing college applications and my future is very bright.

Jacqueline's Story

Growing up, I had been the family's favorite, the first grandchild, cute and smart. All seven of my aunts would always want me to spend time with them. My family had great expectations for me. Life was wonderful—until one week before my sixteenth birthday. I was walking home from school when a man drove by in his car, honked his horn, and called out to me. I ignored him and continued on my way. As I rounded a corner a few blocks later, a man grabbed me. I screamed as he pulled me into his car. I recognized him as the man who had honked at me earlier. He pushed me down onto the fully reclined passenger seat and fastened the seat belt. He warned that if I screamed again or tried to escape, he would kill me. As he drove off, all I could see were the tops of trees and the blue sky. I could also hear the sound of other cars zooming by. I went into survival mode.

"I have herpes, so you don't want to touch me. It's incurable."

"My family will be looking for me!"

I was trying to say anything hoping he would let me go. He hit me and told me to be quiet. I contemplated jumping from the car, but the risk of falling out onto a busy street seemed too great. We drove for what seemed an eternity. Finally, he stopped the car. All I could see were brick walls around us. He pulled out a pouch of white powder and sniffed it. Then he raped me. Out of fear of losing my life, I did everything he asked me to do. Since I was a virgin, it was an extremely painful experience.

Nevertheless, I held back my tears. When the ordeal was over, we just sat there.

Finally, he said, "I really like you. I want to take you out on a date."

"Sure," I said. "But I need to go home and change clothes."

He took my purse and all my identification. He also took down my phone number. I tried to convince him to let me walk home.

"Oh, no," he said. "I'll take you so I'll know where to pick you up later."

As we headed to the area where he had abducted me, he warned me that if I were lying about our date, he would find me and kill me. I directed him to drop me a couple of blocks from my home. When he stopped the car and unlocked the door, I jumped out and ran faster than I had ever run before, leaving everything behind. I got to my house and started kicking and hitting the front door.

"Help me! Help me!"

My mom opened the door looking totally puzzled. I started to tell what had happened; she immediately called the police and other family members. A female police officer came and took me into my bedroom to get my story. As I was talking to the officer, the rapist called on my phone. She took the call, pretended to be me, and arranged a meeting. The man was arrested and charged with kidnapping and rape. He was sentenced to 15 years in prison.

On the second night after the incident, my mother came into my room and told me she did not know how to care for me and that I had to move in with my grandmother. Suddenly,

I lost my status as the family's favorite. No one asked me to visit anymore. I just went numb. I recall having nightmares of the rape. Because I was no longer a virgin, my boyfriend broke up with me. It was the final blow.

I remember thinking, *I will never let another man have control over me sexually again.* Starting very soon after I turned 16, if a boy at school showed me any attention or gave the impression he wanted to have sex with me, I would immediately become the aggressor. I would get him to sleep with me so that I was in control of my body. *If it's my idea, I'm in control.*

I continued this behavior well after high school. I would get together with a man and then soon break up with him before he rejected me. I ended up getting pregnant. Shortly thereafter, I met my husband. Once I married, I had the perfect family. My husband and I had great jobs, our kids were well mannered. We took family vacations, owned a nice home, and were active in church. People regularly complimented us on our model family. My life was finally on track.

But after ten years of marriage, I succumbed to a man's flirtations. I found myself falling into my old post-rape pattern: trying to control what I knew a man wanted from me. I had no physical attraction to this man. And no, he was not filling a void in my marriage. I was happily married. It was all about me being in control of my body. The man I was having the affair with decided to tell my husband—who promptly sought a divorce.

As my life started to fall apart, I was faced with either killing myself or trying to fix the mess I was in. I had destroyed my marriage. My teenage stepkids, whom I'd helped to raise for ten years, did not want to talk to me. My two biological kids now shared a bedroom with me at my brother's home. I had no job and no money. I felt like everyone in my family and church was talking about the affair that ended my ideal marriage. I had lost everything. While I was sitting on the floor in my bedroom, crying and contemplating suicide, a dear friend called me. She helped me realize there was hope.

I took a hard look at the negative patterns in my life. I considered all the people I hated, starting with the rapist. He had taken something that was special to me, something that I wanted to save for my husband: my virginity. He caused me to view sex as a tool to be used to control others, something evil and unrelated to love. He also took my family from me; because of him, my mom gave up on me. I was no longer special to my family. I felt their dreams for me died after the rape. I was just a dirty 15-year-old girl who was no longer a virgin. He'd put me in a humiliating position.

I recalled going to the hospital and getting completely undressed to be examined by a strange doctor. I had to sit in a witness chair in front of a room of strangers and describe the details of what he did to me. He destroyed my life. He was the reason I had yielded my body to so many different men. This man made me walk in fear—fear for my personal safety and that of my kids. Out of fear, I would constantly check the police files to make sure he was still in custody, thinking that when he got out, he would find and kill me. I wanted this man dead. I fantasized about him becoming a victim of rape in prison. I even considered buying a gun so that, once he was released, I could find and kill him myself. It was clear my life was falling apart because of the control this man had over my life, occupying my thoughts 24–7.

I sought counseling. I learned that even though I had loved my husband, I'd used sex as a tool of control. After about six months, I realized that getting my life back on track required me to forgive the man who raped me. I struggled with this for almost a year before I could verbalize it. Then one day I fell to my knees and cried out to the Lord, "I forgive X for sinning against me. He violated my body and destroyed my self-esteem. I release him now." The emotional chains were broken. It was one of the most freeing days of my life. It was like a weight was lifted off my shoulders.

It has been 31 years since the rape. I am not who I used to be. I am at peace. I am now happily remarried and enjoy a healthy, godly relationship with my husband. When I asked the Lord to forgive me and set me free, I became free indeed. The story of my painful, promiscuous past does not make me feel unworthy.

I know deep down inside I have forgiven the man who raped me even though his action started me on a downward spiral. There is no pain or trauma in telling this story. I still get emotional sometimes because of how I almost lost my life—and when I think of the people I have hurt. There is no way I could be where I am today without the grace of the Lord.

Lessons learned

- God loves justice and will see to it that His children are heard and delivered.

- God can make you clean when you surrender your life and your experiences to Him.

- God can heal painful memories and keep us on track for our destiny.

22

Forgiving the Government
A Veteran's Plight

*Let every soul be subject to the governing authorities. For
there is no authority except from God, and the authorities
that exist are appointed by God. Therefore whoever
resists the authority resists the ordinance of God, and
those who resist will bring judgment on themselves.*

ROMANS 13:1-2

Sometimes the choices our government makes can wreak havoc
and even devastation in our lives. Forgiving a government for
its unfair policies is hard because it isn't easy to determine who
is at fault for our pain. Situations are usually complicated and
any efforts for relief can get mired in bureaucratic red tape. The
only person to blame for the negative impact on our lives is usually the top official—the president.

At age 17, Rufus was just another high-school dropout who
couldn't find a job. His uncle, a Vietnam War veteran, encouraged him to go into the military. Rufus's mother and father
thought the structure and discipline would help their son grow
up and take responsibility for himself.

The day after Christmas, Rufus enlisted in the army. Within
three short months, the US went to war with Iraq, and Rufus
was sent to the front to run supplies to troops who were in
combat.

Rufus loved being a soldier. He grew closer to God after a chaplain befriended him and introduced him to a group of young military personnel who were also practicing Christians. One of them was Krista, a pretty young soldier who captured Rufus's heart.

Things seemed to be falling into place for Rufus. "I just knew I was doing God's will," he said. "I thought because I had this special relationship with Jesus that I would be protected."

One day while he was unloading supplies, Iraqi insurgents blew up the truck. Rufus woke up in a hospital confused and in pain. When he looked down, he saw that both of his legs were gone from the knee down.

Soon a hospital chaplain came and told Rufus that Krista had also been injured in the explosion but did not survive. "The grief was overwhelming," Rufus said. "I was numb for days, and then when I realized Krista really wasn't coming back and that I would never be physically whole again, the pain was unbearable."

Soon Rufus was sent home. He went to a Veterans Affairs hospital close to his hometown for rehabilitation. "I was glad to see my family again," he said. "But the grief continued to consume me. I couldn't figure out why God had done this to me."

The hospital always seemed to be short of supplies and staff. Rufus grew frustrated with the amount of time it took to get his prosthetics. "It took months," he said. "Then it seemed like an eternity to get into physical therapy so I could learn to walk again."

The news began reporting that the VA hospitals were not taking care of veterans' needs. Rufus and other Iraq vets began emailing and calling their government representatives about the situation.

"Nothing changed," Rufus said. "Not only did I feel like God had abandoned me, but the government that I had fought and sacrificed for had forsaken me as well." At 21 years old, this was a far cry from the future he had dreamed of.

While he waited for treatment, Rufus continued to meet with the hospital chaplain. His relationship with God began to change. "I realized that God was still with me despite what happened in Iraq," he said. "I understood that I would never know why God didn't prevent that explosion, but that He was still present in my life."

Rufus began helping the chaplain with worship services. During prayer one night, Rufus felt he was being called to ordained ministry. "I'd never thought about being a pastor before," he said, "but I realized that my experiences were leading me to serve God as a preacher and a teacher."

Rufus enrolled in college to study religion. After meeting with his church leaders to fulfill the requirements to become a pastor, he realized that something was holding him back. "I still hated my government," he said. "I was still angry and bitter about the war and the treatment that injured soldiers received when they arrived home. I realized this hatred and bitterness were affecting my relationships with others and with God—and that I had to do something about it."

At his pastor's suggestion, Rufus began journaling about his hatred for the government. He was able to pinpoint why he was so distressed and to see what he had tried to do to make the situation for vets better.

"One day I read through my journal and came to the realization that I had done everything that I could do," he said. "I had no control over whether anything would ever change, but I could take satisfaction in knowing I had done my best to effect the changes I thought needed to happen. I had to let it go and put it in God's hands."

Rufus began praying for the government and for its leaders during his daily devotional. He continued to participate in veterans' programs when he had the time and when he thought he could be useful. "I still needed to do my part to correct the situation," he said. "But my cause didn't have to define me anymore. I was becoming someone different—the leader that God wanted me to be."

Today Rufus is a pastor, a husband, and a father. He's grateful for the trials he experienced in his service to his country, and he has forgiven the government.

Lessons learned

Take steps to forgive an institution that has harmed you by:

- Praying God's blessings upon the institution
- Making a decision not to constantly rehearse the perceived wrong—especially to someone who cannot assist you in effecting change
- Being proactive in trying to change the situation through letter writing or other consciousness raising activities

23

Forgiving a Country and Its People
A Missionary's Nightmare

*"Forgiveness does not change the past, but
it does enlarge the future."*

PAUL BOESE

Connie's Story

My husband and I, along with our two daughters, traveled from
our home in Australia to Ecuador in the late 1980s to serve as
missionaries there. We believed God had called us, so we headed
off on an adventure to change the world for Him.

Our first year there saw our little Ileana added to our family. She struggled with a kidney problem until eventually it was
rectified through surgery. Then she almost drowned, and the
cry of my heart was that God would not take my child from
me. Just one day after that cry to God, when Inez was three and
our middle daughter, Janet, was twelve, both daughters died in
what was a senseless accident with a faulty gas hot water service.

This threw our family into turmoil, and me into a crisis of
faith that lasted a number of years. Once we returned to Australia, I deflected the frequently asked questions about Ecuador by
many who did not know our story, who wanted to know what
it was like for us there.

As far as I was concerned there was no need to return to
Ecuador. Whenever I was asked if we would go back, I always

shrugged and said, "No. There's nothing to go back for. That part of our life is over." I think I still believed that when, 16 years later, God told me it was time to return. It was interesting that God's call to return was to *me* only, not to both my husband and me. I tried to ignore His urging, but He was persistent.

I decided to return for a short-term trip. It wasn't until I was there and the days began to pass, with God bringing people and situations that were both challenging and a blessing, that I could see that perhaps there was a purpose in my going back. I realized at some point (and I can't say exactly when) that, unlike my husband who had accepted what had happened, I held Ecuador responsible for the deaths of Inez and Janet. I held it against the country and the people of Ecuador.

How ironic that God would take me back and allow me to work with Him to bring healing and wholeness to those I considered to be my "enemy" because of what had happened to our children. As I ministered to them, I was ministered to. Forgiveness was intertwined in the healing, and without realizing it, I opened my heart and let the anger, the resentment, and the disdain go.

Just a few days before I was to return home, I was asked to see a lady who was struggling terribly with grief. It was on this day I heard the Holy Spirit whisper to me, *You are bringing healing and hope in a place where you lost hope, where you were wounded so badly, and in turn you are finally healed. Rejoice!*

I began to realize forgiveness is not about glossing over wrongs, or pardoning, condoning, or excusing them. It does not remove the consequences. Our daughters died because the importers of gas heaters removed the safety mechanism that prevented the pilot light from going out. Forgiveness didn't change the fact that our daughters, and others, died because of the actions of those who chose to do something irresponsible and were never held accountable for their actions.

But it did change something in me, and the memory of the harm that was done through their actions lost its power to hurt me anymore.

When Jesus taught the disciples to pray, He taught them what we now know as the Lord's Prayer. Matthew 6:12 in the Amplified Bible says, "And forgive us our debts, as we also have forgiven (left, remitted, and let go of the debts, and have given up resentment against) our debtors." So forgiveness could be defined as the release of resentment and any claims of retribution toward the offender.

When we do this there are a number of benefits. But until God in His gentle way showed me what unforgiveness was doing to me, I had no idea there was a problem. Forgiveness does not remove all the pain, but after forgiveness the pain is bearable. After forgiving you realize that the anger and bitterness had made difficult situations worse, and when grief is involved, these emotions often prevent the mourner from moving forward in their grieving. For me, the act of forgiveness was another step on the path of healing, another step along the trust path as I allowed my heavenly Father to take my hand and lead me on despite the initial difficulty in letting go, of releasing every negative feeling I had toward those I had held responsible for the deaths of our daughters.

Because of that forgiveness, I was able to minister to a lovely Australian lady whose four-year-old daughter was diagnosed with leukemia earlier that year. When the little girl was admitted to the hospital a second time for tests and treatment, her parents were told she would be perfectly all right and would not need to go back to the hospital for five years. Just a few days later the little one died.

By the time I arrived, this devastated mother was struggling so badly that my friend asked if I would see her. As the story unfolded, it became clear that she held unforgiveness toward those who had given her false hope, toward those who prayed for her daughter and told her that God had shown them the little one was healed. There was a strong sense of supernatural presence as we talked during the couple of hours we had together. In such a difficult and memory-provoking situation, I saw God at work using all that had happened to me to minister to another hurting mother. It was a real battle in many ways and exhausting for both of us.

This was a story so near to my own. For God to use this situation as my final time of ministry was a powerful way of showing me that the words He spoke to me one afternoon, so many years before, when I did not want to hear anything He had to say to me, had come to pass: *You can do this; you can use what has happened in your life to help others.* I had come full circle from a place of holding bitterness and anger in my heart to where I could be an instrument of God's love and mercy because unforgiveness was no longer blocking its flow.

Lessons learned

- When God asks us to do something, He also gives us the capacity to obey.

- God is always with us, even in the most difficult times.

- When God leads us somewhere, it is not always about what we can do for Him, but where He can best do in us what He needs to do.

Part 3

Decisions, Decisions
The Forgiveness Process

24

What Forgiveness Is and What It's Not
Debunking the Myths

*"When we forgive evil we do not excuse it, we do not
tolerate it, we do not smother it. We look the evil full
in the face, call it what it is, let its horror shock and
stun and enrage us, and only then do we forgive it."*

LEWIS B. SMEDES

The *New World Dictionary* defines *forgive* as "(1) to give up resentment against or the desire to punish (2) stop being angry with; to pardon (3) to give up all claim to punish or exact penalty for an offense, and (4) to cancel a debt." In this chapter we will look at how to embrace this definition and debunk the myths of what forgiveness is and what it is not.

What Forgiveness Is

Forgiveness is a process that begins with making a series of decisions.

Deciding to accept the reality of the offense. Some people find it hard to accept that a particular person would willfully commit an evil act against them. They search for ways to justify or excuse the action, choosing to blame outside or third-party influences. "Surely my favorite relative didn't betray my confidence." "Mary is too loyal to steal from the company!"

Joseph, having spent 13 years in slavery because of the

actions of his brothers, quickly faced reality when they remorse-fully sought forgiveness: "But as for you, *you meant evil against me*; but God meant it for good" (Genesis 50:20). He made no attempt to justify their awful deed. The process of forgiveness will not begin if we stay in denial and refuse to call the evil what it is.

Deciding to get real about the pain. Sometimes our egos won't allow us to admit that somebody had the power to hurt us—especially when we have a reputation for being a tower of strength, the go-to person in every adversity. We often pretend "that didn't bother me" while dying a million deaths on the inside. Pulling off the mask of invincibility is an act of courage and humility.

Somebody once said, "You can't heal what you won't reveal." When we face our vulnerability and allow ourselves to feel raw human emotions such as disappointment, sadness, or rage, we will be on the road to healing. We don't have to spend precious time beating ourselves up for being in a vulnerable position. Vulnerability is not a sign of weakness but rather a sign of courage. We took the risk of putting our emotions, ideas, finances, and so forth out there not knowing what the results might be. It resulted in pain. We've now learned a valuable life lesson—and it wasn't fatal.

Deciding to let go of all negative emotions. At some point in dealing with a hurt, we must *decide* to let go of the anger, resentment, hate, frustration, or other negative feelings associated with an offense. In so doing, we stop sabotaging our own ability to be forgiven for our trespasses against God and others. "And whenever you stand praying, if you have anything against anyone, forgive him, that your Father in heaven may also forgive you your trespasses. But if you do not forgive, neither will your Father in heaven forgive your trespasses" (Mark 11:25-26).

Deciding to treat the offender like an enemy—Jesus style. "But I say to you, love your enemies, bless those who curse you, do good to those who hate you, and pray for those who spitefully use you and persecute you, that you may be sons of your Father in heaven; for He makes His sun rise on the evil and on the good, and sends rain on the just and on the unjust. For if you love those who love you, what reward have you? Do not even the tax collectors do the same" (Matthew 5:44-46)?

Obviously, these actions are totally contrary to our natural inclinations. Therefore, we will clearly need Divine empowerment to pull them off. What I've learned is to always pray for every offender to come to know Jesus as their Lord and Savior. There is no higher prayer. We can do this. I've provided some sample forgiveness prayers for various offenses in the appendix to get you started.

Deciding to leave vengeance to God. We must stop desiring to see the offender suffer in any way. Here is where we surrender all potential weapons of revenge and our musings about retaliation to the Great Avenger. We come to an understanding that any punishment we mete out personally (as opposed to through the courts) in an effort to gain justice is a violation of Divine Law.

Leaving vengeance to God does not mean that we should not seek justice through a proper judicial process when compensation, punishment, or restitution is in order. For example, I may seek compensation from someone who damaged my property but release any ill will I may feel because they acted irresponsibly. This is simply holding someone accountable for their actions. And even if the courts refuse to rule in my favor, I can choose to forgive the offender.

Deciding to move forward. We were not created to live in two time periods simultaneously—we cannot live effectively in the present with our emotions stuck in the past. We must align every aspect of our being with the present. We decide to stop driving through life looking through the rearview mirror. We are ready to clean the windshield and focus on the vast possibilities ahead.

What Forgiveness Is Not

Many of us are confused about what forgiveness looks like once we make the essential decisions discussed above. Here is what forgiveness is *not*.

An emotion. We must not believe we have not forgiven an offender because we don't have warm, cozy feelings toward them. We have been wounded; wounds need time to heal. While we have stopped entertaining thoughts of revenge, we must remember that forgiveness is a process that may see many relapses and restarts in our emotions. We have to continue to assert our forgiveness until our words form a new pathway of thinking. Soon the old path of unforgiveness, like a no-longer-traveled trail, will fade into oblivion from lack of activity.

A condoning of the offender's behavior. The fact that we've decided to release someone from further obligation does not mean that we are saying their behavior was okay. It is not okay to verbally abuse somebody. It's not okay to borrow money and not repay it. No offensive behavior is okay. Forgiveness looks at such offenses, judges them as wrong, but leaves the resolution of the matter to God. This is not letting the offender off the hook. Rather, it is our conscious and courageous choice to disconnect from the offender, to let ourselves off the hook, and to move forward in freedom.

A tool for running a guilt trip on the offender. We must be careful of the spirit in which we communicate our forgiveness. I admit there have been times when I've said "I forgive you" with an air of spiritual superiority, hoping to make the offender feel ashamed of their actions and to show how "spiritual" I was at this amazingly difficult process.

An automatic restoring of the relationship. Releasing our desire to avenge the wrong is one thing, but to re-embrace someone with the same level of trust we exercised before the transgression is not wise. Yes, the *decision* to forgive must come promptly; trust must be earned back over time. We need to observe actual (versus *promised*) "fruit of repentance," that is, concrete evidence that the offender is making steps to assure the offense will never happen again. We must have the courage to say to the offender, "Prove by the way you live that you have repented of your sins and turned to God" (Luke 3:8 NLT). A willingness to submit to counseling is a good place to start.

Forgetting the offense. Only God can obliterate something from memory—an ability He did not bestow on us humans. Other than sustaining a severe blow to the head or engaging in some form of mind manipulation, chances are we will always remember a hurt. Therefore, we can forget about forgetting. The good news is that our memory is a powerful tool for warning us and protecting us from repeating the mistakes of the past.

When we choose forgiveness, the grace of God enables us to recall the facts of an offense without any desire for retribution.

Lewis B. Smedes was right when he proclaimed, "Forgiving does not erase the bitter past. A healed memory is not a deleted memory. Instead, forgiving what we cannot forget creates a new way to remember. We change the memory of our past into a hope for our future."

25

Disconnecting the Ball and Chain
A 12-Step Forgiveness Strategy

"Forgiveness is not an occasional act, it is a constant attitude."

Martin Luther King Jr.

It seems logical and fair that a person should be punished for perpetrating an injustice against another. For God to require us to forego any retribution simply goes against the grain of our natural inclination. Yet, in His Divine plan, He knows that offenses and hurts are inevitable and that the only way we can have peace is to forgive the offender. It's a tough mandate, but He doesn't expect us to do it in our own strength.

12 Essential Steps to Forgiveness

I applaud anybody who desires to forgive because the desire itself is evidence that God is already at work in a person's heart. "For God is working in you, giving you the desire and the power to do what pleases him" (Philippians 2:13 NLT). Yes, if you are ready to shed that ball and chain of unforgiveness and to free yourself from emotional prison, try these practical steps to victory.

1. Understand that forgiveness is not optional.

Therefore, you can stop your internal debate regarding whether your offenders deserve your mercy or not. Your decision to forgive is simply in obedience to God's command to do so. Further, it determines whether He will forgive your inevitable trespasses against Him and others.

2. Make a list of at least five sins God has forgiven you for.

Here are some often overlooked examples to get you started: envying, gossiping, telling half-truths, stealing time and supplies from your employer, overstating your expenses on your income tax return, flirting with a married man/woman. Now, imagine what the quality of your life would be like if God constantly reminded you of these offenses, required you to spend the rest of your days carrying the guilt of them, and regularly demanded some form of payment but never cancelled your obligation.

3. Recall at least three instances in which someone forgave you.

Perhaps it was the cutting or critical remark you made to your spouse who subsequently expressed his or her forgiveness. Or the time you snapped at your best friend who was only trying to console you or give you wise counsel. If you find it difficult to develop this list, you may have convinced yourself that you didn't really do anything wrong—perhaps because you never apologized—or that because your intentions were not to offend, forgiveness was not warranted. Dear friend, please do not fall into the trap of judging others by their actions but evaluating your own behavior based on your intentions. It's time to not only embrace the Golden Rule of doing unto others as we would have them do unto us, but going a step further and forgiving as others have forgiven you.

4. Make a list of everybody you may be harboring even an inkling of anger and resentment against.

Be sure to include even the people who haven't done anything against you directly but who didn't speak up or help you when you expected them to. Don't exclude anybody from consideration here because of their exalted status (for example, mother, pastor, doctor).

I had to face the fact that I was angry with my dear sweet mother for remaining in a vulnerable position by not seeking more education once she had escaped my father's abuse. She seemed totally devoid of ambition. Exasperated, I kept thinking, *How will you ever empower yourself if you stay economically disadvantaged?* Sometimes, we have to forgive folks (especially close relatives and friends) for making unwise decisions that had no direct impact on us but caused us to worry about them. We will be wise to free them to experience and grow from the consequences of their behavior.

5. Recall at least three people you have already forgiven beyond any doubt.

Just as the young shepherd David recalled his victories over a lion and a bear before he slew Goliath (1 Samuel 17:34-37), I want you to recall your past victories over unforgiveness. This exercise will remind you that you have previous experience in allowing the grace of God to prevail in healing your emotional pain. These are your "lions and bears."

I joyfully share the following list of people (there are several more!) I have totally released:

- my now deceased dad for his domestic violence and always creating an atmosphere of tension that kept the household on edge

- a childhood molester

- a high school friend for getting pregnant by my boyfriend and writing me a nasty letter to gloat about it

- the management of at least three corporations for blatantly discriminating against me (My healing came from Psalm 75:6, which assured me that promotion comes from God alone.)

- a podiatrist for botching my foot surgery and causing permanent damage

- a promoter who ripped off my husband and me for tens of thousands of dollars in an investment scheme (I also forgave myself, as a certified public accountant, for not doing more due diligence and for being too trusting and too busy to pay attention.)

6. Humanize the offender.

Ask God to let you see beyond the offender's hurtful action and to understand their pain. Having empathy will go a long way in softening your feelings and controlling your anger against the monster you've perceived them to be. If given the opportunity, ask the offender to explain what motivated their action. Make every effort to understand the pain and disappointments in their life.

7. Express your pain.

A face-to-face "forgiveness session" with the wrongdoer is preferred, but you may write a letter if you feel this is the only way you will be heard without interruption, if you think the other person may become too emotional or violent, or if they are incarcerated. Although this is not to be a tongue-lashing or guilt-inducing session, you should make every effort to put the depths of your feelings on the table. Know that your true feelings go beyond anger. Identify and express how the offense really made you feel—for example, humiliated, disrespected, betrayed, discriminated against. A good communication model to follow is to say, "When you (describe the specific offense), I felt (a specific emotion)." This step is also effective if the offender has died and you wish to release forgiveness to them.

8. Refuse to be stuck in your story.

There really is no need to rehash your negative past or to use it as an excuse to stay stuck in unforgiveness. Sally, who has dreamed of writing a book for the past 25 years, still resents to this day that her efforts were thwarted by her verbally abusive husband (whom she divorced over 20 years ago) and that she felt trapped by her two young children—both over 30 years old now. Still no progress on the book! She is stuck in her story and won't stop telling it. She refuses to see that her obstacles no longer exist.

9. State your forgiveness.

Say to your offender, "I forgive you for (specific offense) and I free you to live your life without fear of retaliation from me." Caution! You must resist a holier-than-thou attitude as you deliver this line; such pride thwarts *your* spiritual growth. It is also a form of retaliation as its intent is to impose guilt (emotional pain) on the offender.

Notice Joseph's tone when he released forgiveness to his repentant brothers who had sold him into slavery: "'No, don't be afraid. I will continue to take care of you and your children.' So he reassured them by speaking kindly to them" (Genesis 50:21 NLT). Now, I'm not recommending that you walk on eggshells around somebody who has harmed you; I'm simply cautioning you to guard your heart lest you forget that vengeance belongs to God.

Further caution! It is not wise to state your forgiveness to a wrongdoer while you are in a situation where the offenses are ongoing or frequently repeated. Remember that forgiveness is part of a healing process, a decision you make to move forward *after* the hurt. Expressing forgiveness too quickly could very well send a message to the offender that you are a pushover who tolerates abuse and does not request or require change in behavior. You must develop boundaries with appropriate consequences. For example, if your drug-addicted son steals money from your purse, saying "I forgive you" immediately after you discover it would only encourage him to repeat the negative behavior.

10. Refuse to indulge in any pain-masking alternatives.

Do not indulge in any activity (such as eating, shopping, drinking, using drugs, excessive sleeping, sex) designed to dull the pain and keep you from clearly focusing on resolving your unforgiveness. Be honest with yourself and recognize when you have found refuge in an alternative solution.

11. Make a list of lessons learned from the hurt.

Surely you have concluded that, going forward, you would "never again" do this or that. Thank God you are now the wiser. You can join the psalmist in exclaiming,

> My suffering was good for me,
>> for it taught me to pay attention to your decrees.
>> (Psalm 119:71 NLT)

12. Pray a prayer of closure as often as necessary for comfort, strength, and motivation.

Since healing is a process, rest assured that Satan will remind you from time to time of past hurts. You will be ready to do battle as you declare and reaffirm your commitment to moving forward. Here is a sample prayer to get you started. Also, see my prayers for specific offenses in the appendix.

> *Dear Lord, I thank You for Your faithfulness in never leaving me alone. Thank You for the Holy Spirit whom You have sent to walk alongside me to empower me to be more than a conqueror in every situation. I receive Your unconditional love and acceptance. I surrender my pain to You and accept Your peace as I release every person who has ever hurt or disadvantaged me in any way. By faith, I declare that what the enemy meant for bad, You have already turned into good. Therefore, I press on toward the goal for the prize of Your high calling for me. I am free to soar by the power of the Holy Spirit. In the name of Jesus, I pray. Amen.*

26

When to Restore, Redefine, or Release a Relationship

In all your ways acknowledge Him,
and He shall direct your paths.

PROVERBS 3:6

One thing I know for sure: where there are people, there will be offenses that threaten their relationships. We must accept this reality and learn to work through the hurts and wrongs committed against us.

Some people are so afraid of the potential alienation or rejection that often results from confronting an offender, they simply go along to get along. In so doing, they create a relational imbalance they will eventually come to resent. We must realize that conflicts, misunderstandings, and even hurts can be tools for growth in most relationships if the parties practice forgiveness and maintain a strong commitment to effective communication.

Of course, not all offenses are created equal as some have long-term negative consequences. In deciding how to move forward, the offended person must consider whether to reconcile, redefine, or release the relationship.

Restoring a Relationship

An offense does not have to spell the end of a relationship.

Many times people can genuinely hurt or disappoint us without malice aforethought. Consider the friend who spoiled your husband's surprise birthday party when she said to him, "See you Saturday night!" Others may hurt us out of fear or self-promotion, like the coworker who took credit for your idea because the boss had given him an ultimatum to "shape up or ship out." Sometimes people succumb to the temptations of their environment, like the husband who had been faithful the entire 20 years of his marriage, but after an exhausting three months of late nights at the office and fights with his nagging wife about it, he allowed himself to be seduced by a coworker. He'd voluntarily confessed his transgression and assured his wife he did not love the other woman, had no intentions of being with her ever again, and was willing to do whatever was necessary to restore his wife's trust.

The scenarios are endless. I dare not attempt to rank the severity of each offense as only the victim can determine the weight of a hurt. The point is that, when hurt, we have to make a decision to forgive and to choose to go forward with wisdom. If you are at this point in a relationship, consider the following questions to guide your decision:

- What would Jesus do? This sounds trite given the WWJD fad of a few years ago, but really, don't you want to handle this God's way?

- What are the top benefits and enjoyments I derive from my interaction with X and how important are they to me?

- Does X seem genuinely sorry for this transgression?

- If I were to commit a similar offense, how would I want X to respond to me?

- Did I engage in any behavior (even poor or vague communication) that may have encouraged X's action?

Listen folks, humans are human. They make mistakes. You are human; you will make mistakes. This is the reality we must face in every relationship. If you decide to reconcile, please do not sabotage your goal by reminding offenders of what they have done. Yes, discuss the offense, explain how it affected you, agree on a plan of action to avoid a recurrence, and then, let it go.

I'm reminded of the time we had a repair done in our bedroom that required the drywall to be patched. It stuck out like a sore thumb. Unfortunately, we had to repaint the entire room so that the patched area would not be noticeable. Reconciling is like that; you must cover the entire relationship with love and mercy to avoid focusing on the once troubled spot. "And above all things have fervent love for one another, for 'love will *cover* a multitude of sins'" (1 Peter 4:8).

Redefining a Relationship

When you believe there are some redeeming qualities or benefits of continuing a relationship with an offender, then the wisest course of action is to set new boundaries and adopt new expectations. This requires you to assess the person's character and to determine the extent that you are willing to risk further interaction. If Betty has a problem guarding your secrets, then stop sharing them with her. Yes, she may be dependable and will come to your rescue at the drop of a hat, but she has proven she cannot be trusted with your tasty morsels. Face it, Betty has a character flaw that you cannot fix; it's time to redefine the relationship. Going forward, it will be wise to limit your conversations with her to safe topics such as the weather, the latest styles, and popular TV shows.

This is also the best approach to take when you realize that certain people want to use you for the benefits they can get from you. Usually these are close relatives or old friends you desire to stay connected to. Rather than becoming resentful, try setting new boundaries and reducing your expectations. It isn't necessary to announce you have redefined the relationship; just do it. I have relatives who have burned me financially, but I haven't told them "Never again!" I've simply put the wallet away and have a firm no poised for their next request for a bailout.

Releasing a Relationship

Probably the hardest decision to make when you've been hurt is to let the relationship go. Most of us don't like change—even if it's for the better. It's amazing how many people will tolerate an unfulfilling and toxic relationship because it's familiar.

So how do you know when to let go? Here are ten signs that it may be time to move on:

1. You dread interacting with the person.

2. You feel depleted or drained after you have been together.

3. You are not free to be yourself; you must compromise your core values, beliefs, or personality to walk in harmony with the person.

4. The person verbally abuses or belittles you, or makes you the butt of their jokes.

5. You rationalize that being with the person is better than being alone.

6. The person is selfish or inflexible regarding your outings or always expects you to treat.

7. You have expressed your hurt, but the person continues to repeat the negative behavior.

8. The person has no interest in or regard for your dreams, goals, or preferences.

9. You tolerate the person's offenses only because you need the financial security he provides.

10. You know in your innermost being that the relationship is toxic and God is not pleased with it.

I pray, dear friend, that if any of the above is true regarding your relationship, you will ask God for the grace to let it go. And yes, you must inform the person that you have decided to let go. God will give you the script. Here's one to get you started: "I believe God is calling me to pursue a different path for my life. I must obey Him. I pray that He will give you clear directions for your future." This statement is clear and needs no further explanation.

Now, if the offender is your spouse, you'll want to seek

marriage counseling rather than unilaterally disconnecting from the relationship. Also, remember that people can change, and at some point you may want to reconsider your decision to release the relationship. When John Mark deserted the apostle Paul and Barnabas on their first missionary trip, Paul wrote him off and would not consent to taking him on a second trip:

> Then after some days Paul said to Barnabas, "Let us now go back and visit our brethren in every city where we have preached the word of the Lord, and see how they are doing." Now Barnabas was determined to take with them John called Mark. But Paul insisted that they should not take with them the one who had departed from them in Pamphylia, and had not gone with them to the work. Then the contention became so sharp that they parted from one another. And so Barnabas took Mark and sailed to Cyprus; but Paul chose Silas and departed, being commended by the brethren to the grace of God (Acts 15:36-40).

Sometime later, however, we find that Paul had a change of heart and instructed Timothy to "get Mark and bring him with you, for he is useful to me for ministry" (2 Timothy 4:11). Paul, no longer viewing Mark as a useless deserter but rather as a useful minister, decided to restore the relationship. Yes, stay open to the fact that people change and that God requires us to "love mercy" (Micah 6:8).

27

Seeking Forgiveness
When You Are the Offender

Blessed is he whose transgression is forgiven,
whose sin is covered.

PSALM 32:1

Although the focus of this book is on forgiving people who have hurt or offended us, inevitably, we will offend or hurt another person and we too will need to ask to be forgiven. Adam Hamilton, author of *Forgiveness: Finding Peace Through Letting Go*, explains it this way:

> Forgiveness is essential to our lives. Without it, no marriage can survive, no family can stay together, and no society can be sustained. It is a necessary part of lasting friendships and work relationships. The reason lies in an inescapable fact of human nature: we are bound to hurt others, and others are bound to hurt us. If we are to live successfully, and if we are ever to know freedom and joy, these six words must be a regular part of our vocabulary: "I am sorry" and "I forgive you." If we lack the ability to say, "I am sorry," life will be immeasurably more difficult than it needs to be. If we can't bring ourselves to say, "I forgive you," life will be filled with bitterness and pain.[9]

This chapter is about how to say "I'm sorry," how to express our remorse and our desire for a more positive relationship going forward. In my book *30 Days to Taming Your Kid's Tongue*, I presented guidelines for parents to teach children how to deliver an effective apology. These guidelines are based on Psalm 51—the passage King David wrote to God after he slept with Bathsheba and had her husband killed to hide the resulting pregnancy (2 Samuel 11). Although that book is targeted toward children, many adults also do not know how to ask for forgiveness. Some do it ineffectively, beginning with such statements as "If I did anything to hurt or offended you…" or they shortcut the process with a simple "I'm sorry."

Listen folks, when you have inflicted pain on someone, they often need you to massage their wounded emotions with humble, soothing, caring, repentant words. A terse "Sorry" is simply inadequate. If you are truly sorry, then you'll be willing to do whatever it takes to convince the person of your sincerity. I've heard some men say, "I'm just not the mushy type." Then step outside your comfort zone, sir, and get busy. You'll want to seek God's wisdom for your script to assure the best results:

> It is the same with my word.
>   I send it out, and it always produces fruit.
> It will accomplish all I want it to,
>   and it will prosper everywhere I send it.
> You will live in joy and peace.
>   The mountains and hills will burst into song,
>   and the trees of the field will clap their hands!
>   (Isaiah 55:11-12 NLT)

Remember that being sorry is an expression of your regret and remorse. When you say, "I'm sorry," you focus on the pain or inconvenience you caused the other person. The following guidelines have worked for me for the past few decades:

Ask God's forgiveness first since all sin is a sin against Him. "Against You, You only, have I sinned, and done this evil in Your sight" (Psalm 51:4). Allow the Holy Spirit to convict you of your sin so that you come with a penitent heart.

Assess your objective in asking for forgiveness. Do you really want to express true sorrow for your actions or is the objective to avoid guilt or negative consequences? Be genuine in your motive. Manipulation is often easy to discern and it's ungodly.

Approach the wounded person as soon after the offense as possible. Allowing too much time to pass only allows people to make more assumptions about your motives or intentions.

Admit the specific offense. An effective apology acknowledges your hurtful action. ("I apologize for raising my voice at you in the store." "I shouldn't have used your car without your permission.")

Acknowledge your remorse. ("I'm so sorry. I feel really bad about this because I know how important it is to you.") Don't try to minimize the impact of your actions by saying such things as "I don't know why you are making such a big deal over this."

Accept full responsibility. ("I take responsibility for my actions." "It was very irresponsible/inconsiderate/selfish of me to _____.") Don't make excuses or blame anyone else—especially the victim. "If you hadn't done Y, I would not have done Z."

Ask for forgiveness. "Please forgive me." Just saying these words is a humbling act. Hearing them puts the victim in a more receptive position. That person has a choice now; they are not powerless.

Assure a change in behavior. ("It won't happen again. Here's what I'm willing to do in the future to avoid a recurrence.") Be specific about the behavioral change you have already made or are willing to make to show evidence of your true change of heart.

Make amends where possible. ("I'm willing to do _____ to make you whole, to cover this loss." "I'm willing to be accountable to _____ to show my deep desire for change.")

Caution: If the person you have hurt doesn't respond favorably, don't push it. Emotional wounds, like physical wounds, do not heal overnight. Give that person time to process their pain. Don't remind them that God commands them to forgive. Their obedience is between them and God.

I dated a young man once who didn't show up for a date or two—and did not apologize. I was furious. Adding insult to injury, he accused me of not being a "good Christian" because I was supposed to overlook his inconsiderateness and forgive him. I refused to respond to his guilt tactics. I set firm boundaries with clear consequences. The last time he stood me up for a date, I had already decided to move on emotionally. Seven months later, I married my husband of 36 years!

Part 4

Forgiveness Is Good for You
Exploring the Benefits and Rewards

28

Spiritual Rewards
Preserving the Connection to the Almighty

> *"And whenever you stand praying, if you have anything*
> *against anyone, forgive him, that your Father in heaven*
> *may also forgive you your trespasses. But if you do not forgive,*
> *neither will your Father in heaven forgive your trespasses."*

MARK 11:25-26

Mount Wilson is one of the highest peaks in the Los Angeles area, reaching over a mile above sea level. Most of the local TV stations have their broadcast antennas there. Even households without cable television can get great TV reception from these stations since nothing interferes with the transmission of the signal.

I often think of forgiving as mountaintop living. When we decide we will not allow unforgiveness to interfere with our ability to hear from God, to receive his "transmissions" (instruction, warnings, encouragement), we experience a higher level of living—the level God intended. After all, He "raised us up together, and made us sit together in the heavenly places in Christ Jesus" (Ephesians 2:6). I like to imagine myself seated high above the offenses, disappointments, and hurts that can banish me to the low ground of unforgiveness. Unhindered communication from God, then, is one of the first spiritual benefits that come to mind.

Second, since communication is a two-way street, we want to make sure that we not only hear from God, but we want to know He also hears and will answer our prayers. Unforgiveness will not merely *hinder* our prayers; it will block them due to unforgiven sin.

"But wait," you may exclaim. "I asked forgiveness for my sins." Well, sorry, but if you haven't forgiven others, your sins are still unforgiven according to Mark 11:25-26. Now you can see why it's spiritual suicide to hold on to offenses.

Third, not only does forgiveness position us for clear two-way communication with our heavenly Father, it is a sure pathway to peace of mind—the peace that comes from knowing we have obeyed His command. The psalmist proclaimed, "righteousness and peace have kissed" (Psalm 85:10). Yes, there is an intimate connection between experiencing the peace of God and doing the right thing. Forgiving is the right thing to do; we have the power to do it. Just as we are saved by the grace of God, we forgive by the grace of God.

Last, unforgiveness keeps us from walking in the Spirit. When we languish in negative emotions fueled by past hurts, our carnal nature rules us. But a decision to forgive acts as a counteracting force.

Even Jesus had to make the choice to forgive in order to complete God's ultimate plan of salvation for all. Just imagine what the world would be like today had Jesus chosen to use His Divine power to punish everyone who laid a hand on Him or who participated in any way in His crucifixion. Rather than retaliating, He forgave. After Peter cut off the ear of the high priest's servant, Jesus reminded him of the power He had available to Him if His goal had been to retaliate: "Do you think that I cannot now pray to My Father, and He will provide Me with more than twelve legions of angels?" (Matthew 26:53).

Imagine the power it took to forgive such an enormous offense. Jesus forgave every Pharisee, Sadducee, Roman soldier, man, and woman who cursed Him, spat in His face, plucked His beard, or abused Him in any way. Because of His decision to walk in the perfect will of His heavenly Father, His spiritual line of communication with His Father was never broken.

The apostle Paul admonished, "Walk in the Spirit, and you shall not fulfill the lust of the flesh" (Galatians 5:16). Forgiving those who have hurt us is a part of walking in the Spirit.

Edward's mother passed away several years ago after a nine-month battle with a rare cancer. It was very difficult for Edward to watch such a strong woman succumb to the decaying effects of the disease. At the lowest point of his life, he turned away from God, angry over his sudden loss. Walking apart from God, he temporarily lost the ability to discern right from wrong. His life was spiraling out of control. It was only when Edward's marriage came close to ending that he halted his destructive path and surrendered his life fully to God. Part of that process was asking forgiveness for what he did not understand as part of God's plan. Edward had to come to the place where he recognized his grievance was against God Himself. In so doing, he turned over his rage, opening his heart to receive God's love and instruction.

There really is no ambiguity when it comes to spiritual matters. The message is clear—we are either walking with God in His love and direction or we are walking in the flesh, leaning on our own understanding. Choosing to hold a grudge against someone only stunts our spiritual growth as we disobey God's Word and channel our energy and efforts in the wrong direction. We have to forgive in order to grow spiritually. A son has to forgive an absentee father. A wayward daughter needs to forgive her emotionally cold mother. Brothers must forgive each other for past transgressions. Sisters must forgive offenders for wrongs previously committed.

If the spiritual pathway to God's grace and mercy can be viewed as a four-lane highway, then a grudge is the equivalent to gridlock. The path from point A to point B is halted by the traffic jam of vengeful thoughts, anger, rage, and false fears implanted by Satan. However, forgiveness clears away the wreckage and clutter, freeing all lanes and reopening the pathway to spiritual growth.

Forgiveness gives us a clear channel to God. It is essential for our spiritual well-being.

29

Emotional Benefits
Paving the Path to Inner Peace

*"I will not permit any man to narrow and
degrade my soul by making me hate him."*

BOOKER T. WASHINGTON

From early manhood, Nelson Mandela protested the indignities of the South African apartheid government that treated people differently based on their race. He was sentenced to life in prison in 1963 on charges of attempting to overthrow the state. After 27 years of domestic and international protests, he was finally released. He chose to forgive his captors. "As I walked out the door toward the gate that would lead to my freedom, I knew if I didn't leave my bitterness and hatred behind, I'd still be in prison."

Mandela went on to become the country's first democratically elected president and the winner of the 1993 Nobel Peace Prize. Even in his later years, he spoke around the world, challenging people to forgive each other because it was the right thing to do for spiritual and emotional freedom.

Mattie told me her story of finding emotional freedom when she chose God's way.

Mattie's Story

As far back as I can remember, my parents taught my siblings and me the Scriptures on forgiveness. However, it was the forgiveness they regularly *demonstrated* that had the most impact on us. They were remarkable people. They led a strong Christ-centered ministry in our city and enjoyed worldwide influence. Renowned leaders sought their counsel.

My parents seemed to have an abundance of love and ability to forgive. They cared about the whole person and helped others build good character and behavior. While they were not perfect, they served a perfect God and allowed Him to use their lives. Whenever detractors tried to find fault with the ministry or their character, they would stand firm in their faith and refuse to defend themselves or to retaliate. They toiled tirelessly building and perfecting the people entrusted to their care. However, all the years of service took their toll on my father's health. After his sixtieth birthday, he had a massive stroke. The doctors did not expect him to live. It seemed like the sky had fallen. But the congregation and their worldwide support system prayed!

My mother and father had been a strong capable team together, and Mom had no desire to serve as a solo senior pastor. She worked hard to nurture my dad back to health as well as fill the role of pastor. She would spend nights in tears asking God to intervene. Her strong earthly arm had been greatly weakened and she didn't want to carry the full weight of the ministry.

A friend recommended that the church hire a young, up-and-coming preacher I'll call Jack to join the ministerial staff. My mom and dad loved and treated him like a son. They decided to step down as senior pastors, choosing to serve as pastors emeriti. They encouraged their congregation to embrace Jack as their spiritual leader. He, in turn, promised to honor and support my parents and to lead his new congregation with humility and care.

Initially, the transition moved forward smoothly. Jack was an anointed preacher and the Word of God flowed through him mightily. My parents' backing and endorsement opened many ministry doors for him and his young family. He was readily accepted into pastoral circles because people trusted the word of my parents. He quickly became known nationally and internationally. However, after a while, Jack's attitude changed toward my parents, and he refused to keep certain promises he had made to them.

When you are the son or daughter of a pastor, you observe the upside and the downside of ministry up close and personal. But to watch your parents being mistreated is an extremely hard pill to swallow. When you know how they have served and loved thousands of people out of a pure heart rather than a desire for money, it really hurts. I began to question, "Where is God in this? Why is He allowing this?" Several members were aware of the ill treatment and alienation of my parents. They wanted to fight back. My sisters and our husbands wanted to fight back. Family and friends wanted to fight back. We wanted to take legal action to enforce certain agreements that affected my parents' livelihood. But my mother wouldn't hear of it. She insisted that we allow God to handle it.

During this time, my mother's personal ministry began to revive. She was once again invited to speak around the world. However, due to my father's health, she accepted invitations only within the US. Those close to them knew the inequities they had suffered. We saw how years of ministry and the pain of loss weighed heavily upon them. They walked in forgiveness, but they were still hurting.

My mother began to experience physical pain. She had a cold that wouldn't go away. She had a knee wound that would not heal. Her body ached and her strength was waning. However, she pressed on.

In 1993, my parents decided they needed to go away for an extended rest. They went to my father's favorite vacation spot, Hawaii. While there, my mother had to be rushed to the emergency room on Thanksgiving Day. After several tests and X-rays, the doctors informed her that she had lung cancer.

They flew home the next day. Subsequent tests revealed the cancer had metastasized to her bones. The doctors marveled that she was functioning as well as she was. Approximately five months after her diagnosis, my mother became paralyzed from the chest down. We ordered a hospital bed, and family and friends, along with hospice nurses, cared for her around the clock. My mother's mind remained sharp. Her love for God remained firm. Her ability to forgive became even more evident.

One day my mother and father requested that Jack come to see them. When he came, they poured more love into him. My mother said with compassion, "Son, if we have in any way offended you or brought shame to you, please forgive us. We love you like a son and want God to use and bless you."

"I forgive you," he responded. "I know that I have not done anything to you or said anything about you. But if you think I have, I'm sorry."

My sister and I were nearby and heard the conversation. My mother had given us strict orders, "Don't say a word!" We certainly had some choice things we would have said if she hadn't ordered us to keep silent. I couldn't understand this kind of love and forgiveness. Our mother was just too nice. We were angry and hurting, but God held our tongues.

My parents passed away within a few years of each other with Mom making her transition first. Afterward, God began to deal with me about my relationship with Him. One day He said, "Mattie, it's time." I knew exactly what He meant. I loved God, but I was still wrestling with unforgiveness. I could not let go of how Jack had mistreated my parents. I needed emotional healing.

One day I saw him on a Christian television program. An overwhelming feeling of love and forgiveness poured over me. I knew the Holy Spirit was at work and that the forgiveness process had begun. I prayed for him and his family. I saw him several more times on television, and each time I felt warmer toward him. I constantly verbalized my forgiveness. It took several months for me to feel complete emotional healing and to know that I had fully forgiven. But I knew it had happened! I was already feeling free emotionally.

The final exam occurred when I came face-to-face with him at a celebration at my parents' former church. The seating arrangement forced me to come directly across his path. I embraced him; I felt no ill will whatsoever. It was indeed a supernatural moment. Thank God, my parents taught me *how* to forgive. Thank God, the Holy Spirit enabled me to do it.

Once we decide to let go of the pain, anger, bitterness, and resentment, the Holy Spirit will give us the willingness to forgive the person who has wronged us. Only then will we experience true peace and emotional freedom—freedom to pursue His purpose for our life.

30

Physical Rewards
Mastering Resentment, Maintaining Health

*"We must be saved by the final form of
love, which is forgiveness."*

REINHOLD NIEBUHR

The act of forgiveness can literally take a load off your chest. So says Dr. Fred Luskin, director of the Stanford Forgiveness Project. In his bestselling book, *Forgive for Good, A Proven Prescription for Health and Happiness,* he reports that several research studies found that just the mere *idea* of forgiving someone allowed some people to feel better. On the other hand, if the participants in the study *imagined* themselves as unforgiving, they had negative reactions, such as high blood pressure. Throughout the book, he explains that people who are more forgiving report fewer symptoms of stress and health problems. Failure to forgive may be more significant than hostility as a risk factor for heart disease.[10]

We can go a long way in promoting our general health just by choosing to forgive. Unforgiving people keep themselves in a constant state of tension by thinking often about the situation and people involved in a transgression. Such chronic tension can lead to depression and hopelessness.

Why allow offenders to rent free space in our heads and control the quality of our lives by focusing on them? We can choose to avoid the stress and tension associated with reliving the hurtful situation—when we choose to forgive.

Ellen's Story

My aunt Ruby was the wife of my mother's brother Jerry. She was like my second mother. She never had children of her own, so she directed a lot of her love and attention to my sister and me. We would cheerfully run errands for her and take care of whatever chores she asked of us. As the years went by, I got closer to Aunt Ruby because our family moved in with her and Uncle Jerry for a little while when things got tough.

Aunt Ruby took special care to let me know how much I meant to her. I was like the daughter she never had. "I own some property," she once told me, "and I'm going to pass it on to you for your financial security. It's a large parcel and it will help to give you a good start in life." I was delighted at Aunt Ruby's kindness and generosity toward me. I promised her that I would take care of her gift and that I would not let her down.

You can imagine my shock and grief when Aunt Ruby passed away suddenly just as I turned 19. I later learned that as her health began to decline, she had appointed Jerry to oversee her financial affairs according to the wishes she expressed in her will. This included bequeathing the property to me.

Jerry refused to discuss the matter with me. He denied that Ruby left a will or had expressed any desire to pass on the property to me. He banned me from attending any family meetings. This situation became contentious within our extended family because several of my cousins confided in me that they had seen Ruby's will. They did not want to confront Jerry because they feared retribution.

I was shocked that my uncle, my blood relative, could do such a terrible thing to me. He was already a wealthy man, and I couldn't believe he would defraud his own niece. His dishonesty affected the course of my life, and I was bitter about it.

As the years went by, I became more and more bitter, particularly when I was faced with financial challenges. I wanted justice. I wanted vengeance. I didn't want anything to do with him. He could rot for all I cared.

I knew that Jerry didn't like me much. He resented my family because he didn't have children of his own. He often directed his resentment toward my mother, who had five children. He even asked my mother to relinquish her parental rights to my youngest sibling so that he could adopt her. He finally found a way to get back at me by stealing my inheritance.

I wanted Uncle Jerry to pay for his misdeeds. I wanted him to suffer for what he did to me, and I often fantasized about having him beat up. Although I never followed through on my thoughts, I got a certain amount of pleasure just thinking of it. I cut him out of my life completely. As far as I was concerned, he had been removed from the face of the earth.

Years later I got the news I had waited for—Jerry had died. When I heard, I laughed. Yes, I did! *Good for the scoundrel, he finally got what he deserved.* I didn't attend his funeral because my bitterness and unforgiveness toward him still consumed me.

But as I looked back, I understood that my unforgiveness came at a high price. I paid with physical ailments. I developed rheumatoid arthritis and scleroderma. My days and nights were filled with pain. I began to realize if I wanted the quality of my life to improve, I had to come to terms with the resentment I held toward Jerry even after his death. Letting go was tough, but

I soon recognized that forgiving him was a gift to myself; I could no longer afford to hold on to these feelings because they were destroying my body.

I began to face up to the role that unforgiveness had played in my life. It held me in an emotional prison for over 20 years. To move forward, I'd need to eradicate it from my life. One day, while in prayer, I made the decision—I would release Jerry from his debt to me. I had to release him because my mind and body were going through too much pain, so I verbalized it, "Uncle Jerry, I forgive you"…and I meant it.

Today I rarely think about this offense—and I'm a much happier person. I have been relieved of my emotional pain. My health has improved dramatically. My pastor played a tremendous role in helping me to forgive by teaching several lessons on forgiveness. I came to realize I was not perfect and that I also needed forgiveness from those I may have unknowingly hurt. I made the decision to "forgive as I was forgiven." Now I make it a practice to forgive right away. I have learned that harboring ill feelings can be devastating to my physical health. If I were to write a title for my story of unforgiveness, I would call it "My Body Can't Afford It."

31

Relational Rewards
Extending Compassion, Abandoning Anger

*"Forgiveness is the economy of the heart. Forgiveness saves the
expense of anger, the cost of hatred and the waste of spirits."*

ROBERT MULLER

"Lord, please help me," the husband said. "I don't want to be
angry anymore. I just can't forgive her." But in time, he did forgive her. Their marriage strengthened beyond his imagination
after surviving the fiery trial. Forgiveness freed him to love her
despite her human failures.

"I hate my dad," the daughter exclaimed. "If he dies tonight, I
won't shed a single tear." But she shed many tears when his heart
suddenly stopped, and doctors performed emergency proce-
dures to revive him. That night, she prayed for another chance
to make things right between them. Seven years later, he walked
her down the aisle and turned her over to the care of his new
son-in-law.

"God, I want him to pay for what he did to me," Sally prayed
as the tears flowed down her cheeks, recalling the night she was
violated by a trusted friend. When the Lord placed the command to forgive on her heart, she ignored it. Not long afterward,
she discovered he'd been arrested on a similar charge and sentenced to several years in jail. There was no celebrating on her
part. In fact, she took a bus ride to the county jail and visited her

former friend. During their conversation, he broke down and apologized for what he'd done to her. He explained how he had been the victim of abuse at a young age. She forgave him. Today, 30 years later, their friendship is stronger than ever.

Perhaps you know someone carrying a huge chip on their shoulder and having a hard time relating to others. Everyone is capable of expressing sentiments similar to these due to the bitter seed of sin that lies deep within our hearts. Unfortunately, we are born with it, destined to cultivate it naturally, as men and women of a fallen world. Godly traits such as compassion, sacrifice, and forgiveness do not automatically appear in our character because of our fallen nature. We have to become intentional in showing compassion. Self-sacrifice has to be taught because we will naturally look out for ourselves before helping anyone else. Forgiveness requires us to not only give others a pass on past hurts, but to love them despite the pain they may have caused us.

Perhaps you have experienced the relational trauma of an absent father, an abusive mother, a best friend who let you down, a work partner's ugly words spoken against you. Maybe your favorite cousin laughed at you behind your back. Perhaps a boyfriend betrayed your trust.

Whatever the situation may have been, there are people in our lives who have or will let us down. Our first instinct is to put that person on the "distrust list." Or even to play God and banish them from our presence forever. Sometimes, the offense is so horrible, we entertain thoughts of vengeance and retribution against them. This is the state of mind where our natural inclinations take over and produce a fleshly craving of unforgiveness.

Unforgiveness poisons the mind, binds the heart, and often sets us on the destructive path of revenge—or at least obsessive thoughts of it. The world tells us that revenge is a dish to be savored, and far too many people subscribe to that mantra.

But unforgiveness only succeeds in holding *one* person captive. Chances are the deadbeat dad doesn't care about how angry his estranged daughter is. The burglar who stole your iPhone has already forgotten you and moved on to another target. The cheating boyfriend who left you for your best friend has justified his decision and gone his merry way with no regard for your feelings.

Nevertheless, many people, seething in hate, hold out for that day when retribution will be duly served. Some contemplate imaginary scenarios and situations that are doomed to never be. In short, they waste precious time that could be used enjoying today. The antidote to this dilemma is to call upon the Holy Spirit and accept His empowering grace to walk in love.

Jesus knew He was destined for an unspeakable death but willingly went to the cross for us anyway. He died so that we might be forgiven of our sins, once and for all. In so doing, He modeled perfectly what compassion, sacrifice, and forgiveness should look like.

Think about it. Jesus has every right to turn His back on us because of our constant disobedience to Him. Instead, He continues to be a living model of the statement, "Love your neighbor as yourself." By loving us, He opens the way for us to get to know Him better. By forgiving our sins, God gives us the opportunity to develop a healthy relationship with Jesus. That's what He wants, and the same applies to us. When we forgive, we are set free of hatred and pain. That freedom allows us to not only move forward in life, but it also may open the door for a new or stronger relationship between ourselves and our offenders.

Tito and Charles were bitter enemies who often fought as adolescents. At the center of their hostile relationship was Dawn, who dated both boys off and on. She eventually settled for Charles, further aggravating Tito. But at some point in his life, Tito turned his life over to Jesus. When that happened, one of the first burdens he laid down was his bitter resentment toward Charles. The day came when the two young men sat down to discuss their tense relationship, and Tito apologized for contributing to the hostility between them and asked Charles for forgiveness.

At first, Charles didn't know what to make of the situation, but he reluctantly accepted Tito's request. The two men slowly developed a brand-new relationship built on the foundation of love and forgiveness. When Charles was water-baptized 18 years later, Tito sat in the front row of the church and supported his best friend. After 22 years, the two men still have a thriving friendship.

That's the power of God working through forgiveness. Relationships are cultivated when hatred and fear are laid to rest. Hebrews 12:14-15 (esv) warns, "Strive for peace with everyone, and for the holiness without which no one will see the Lord. See to it that no one fails to obtain the grace of God; that no 'root of bitterness' springs up and causes trouble, and by it many become defiled."

We can't even develop a right relationship with the Lord if we harbor unforgiveness within our hearts.

32

Financial Rewards
Releasing the Debt, Reaping the Return

"And forgive us our debts,
as we forgive our debtors."

MATTHEW 6:12

A man called our office several years ago to order a book for a friend. He didn't own a credit card but explained that time was of the essence. His friend needed the book right away. He promised to put the check in the mail the same day. After sharing some very personal details about her plight, he asked me not to reveal his identity when sending her the book.

I shipped the book to his friend in good faith. He never sent the money—despite at least five follow-up calls. I kept the invoice in my "Unpaid Invoices" file for several years. Each time I saw the invoice, even though the amount due was under $20, I'd feel a little enraged. How dare somebody be so financially irresponsible? How could he take advantage of my kindness? I thought of sending his friend a letter and letting her know all the personal things he had said about her—as well as the fact that he'd never paid for the book.

One day, as I was reviewing the outstanding invoices, I felt the Holy Spirit's nudging. "Let it go. Toss the unpaid invoice and release the man from any further obligation."

"But Lord, he ripped me off. I can't let him off the hook like that. It's the principle of the thing!"

I'm ashamed to admit that it took me several months after that to shred the invoice. After I finally released the deadbeat from any future obligation, I felt a sense of calm. I hadn't realized that the unforgiven debt was stealing my peace of mind, stifling my creativity, and keeping me from moving forward. I needed to move away from Shouldville, where people honored their debts as they should. I needed to give up all hope for a different past.

Several years later, I hired a local fashion designer to make a couple of outfits. He insisted that I pay in full in advance. When I went to pick up the garments, he had totally messed them up, and the design could not be corrected due to the unique cut. He admitted, in the presence of my assistant, that this was not his best work, and he promised to remake the outfits when he returned from an extended trip.

I never got a stitch of clothing—or a refund of the significant sum I'd paid. I could have taken him to small-claims court, but I chose not to. I refused to be stuck in unforgiveness on this debt even though it was much higher than the $20 book invoice. I found comfort in the words of the psalmist:

> Rest in the LORD, and wait patiently for Him;
> Do not fret because of him who prospers in his way,
> Because of the man who brings wicked schemes to pass.
> Cease from anger, and forsake wrath;
> Do not fret—it only causes harm.
> For evildoers shall be cut off;

> But those who wait on the LORD,
> They shall inherit the earth.
> (Psalm 37:7-9)

I find it fascinating that Jesus used a financial parable to demonstrate the principles of forgiveness. In Matthew 18:23-35, he relates that a certain king had made loans to several of his servants and decided it was time for them to settle their accounts. One servant, whom I will call X, owed him an amount that was way beyond his ability to repay. The king commanded that he and his family be sold into slavery to settle the debt. X begged the king to be patient with him and give him more time. Moved by X's plea, the king showed compassion and simply forgave the debt, leaving X free to go.

X then found one of his fellow servants, Y, who owed him a fraction of the debt the king had just forgiven. X grabbed Y by the throat and demanded immediate repayment. Even though Y begged for more time, the unmerciful X refused to grant it. He had Y thrown into jail until he could repay the debt.

The other servants witnessed the whole scene and reported it to the king. He was furious! He gave X a scathing rebuke, rescinded his decision to forgive the debt, and sent him to prison to be tortured until he paid his huge obligation. Jesus concluded the parable by warning, "That's what my heavenly Father will do to you if you refuse to forgive your brothers and sisters from your heart" (Matthew 18:32-35 NLT).

Yes, unforgiveness can sentence you to an emotional prison where you will be tormented with thoughts of the loss or inequity you have suffered until you decide to let it go. When you let go, you free your mind to receive God's creative ideas and to be more productive.

In his groundbreaking book, *How to Forgive When You Can't*, Dr. Jim Dincalci reported the results of a study in which salesmen who had a one-day workshop on forgiveness and emotional competence, as well as regular forgiveness coaching over a six-month period, sold two-and-a-half-times more than their coworkers who had none of this training.[11] Yes, forgiveness is good for you financially!

Perhaps someone has burned you in a financial transaction. What's worse, the perpetrator has the financial wherewithal to repay the debt (or at least a part of it) but has gone his merry way. This can be infuriating. I've been burned financially several times. Somehow, I've found it easier to release a relational offense than a financial one. Perhaps, it's because in most cases where someone has caused a nonfinancial injury, there is no tangible repayment. But when it comes to financial matters, the perpetrator could make you whole in most cases but chooses not to—leaving you feeling ripped off, violated, disadvantaged, powerless…and motivated to avenge the wrong.

Be of good cheer, dear reader; do not fret. This situation can work for your good as you let go of your negative thoughts. Yes, seek recompense through legal channels if feasible, but don't get stuck in the anger. Don't allow the loss to dictate the quality of the rest of your life. Decide to set yourself free from your debtor.

Learn from the burn, but forgive to live!

Epilogue

Forgiving Is Supernatural

It's time to give up all hope for a better *past*. It's time to see the pain in your history as "His story"—for you. Yes, God knew the story of your life before you were conceived.

> You saw me before I was born.
> Every day of my life was recorded in your book.
> Every moment was laid out
> before a single day had passed.
> (Psalm 139:16 NLT)

In God's grand scheme for your life, He *allowed* an offender to take something from you—your dignity, your job, your spouse, your peace, your innocence, your dreams, your mobility, your expectations, your prized possession. The list is endless.

But be of good cheer! God is a restorer and He has made you more than a conqueror through Christ Jesus, the most renowned champion of forgiveness of all time. He endured the brutal indignities of a crucifixion and offered a prayer for His transgressors from the cross, "Father, forgive them, for they do not know what they do" (Luke 23:34).

Yes, history has provided many awesome examples of famous and ordinary people who chose to forgive. I believe it's time to count you in that number. It's time to forgive all who have transgressed against you.

No doubt you have concluded from the stories in this book that forgiving others does not come naturally. Perhaps you struggle with the belief that forgiving a wrongdoer is a violation of an unwritten moral code that people should be punished for their injustices to others. After all, life must be fair.

Although it seems that some people can indeed let go of hurts easier than others, know that even they do not possess an *inherent* ability to forgive. Forgiveness is a work of grace, a Divine enabling to obey God's command. I am reminded of the words of my spiritual mentor, "God never gives us a responsibility without giving us the ability to respond." When it comes to releasing our debtors, we can find comfort in knowing that the Holy Spirit walks alongside to empower us to fulfill God's commands.

Forgiveness takes practice. We can begin to be better forgivers by releasing the sting of small infractions, insults, and cutting remarks. We can resist the temptation to hold a grudge. In Horatio Palmer's hymn "Yield Not to Temptation," he writes,

> Yield not to temptation, for yielding is sin;
> Each vict'ry will help you some other to win.

Yes, we can strengthen our "forgiveness muscle" with practice, practice, practice—empowered by the Holy Spirit.

You are now at a point of decision. I hope this book has inspired you to make that big step to spiritual and emotional freedom. What will you do? Keep holding on to that hot coal of hatred and bitterness until it consumes you? Or will you cast it before the Lord and let him soothe your pain, heal your wounds, and finish "His story" for your life.

The choice is yours. He is waiting to turn your ashes into beauty.

Forgiveness Prayers
for Life's Hurts
and Injustices

Rejected

Father, You created every person as free moral agents with the power of choice; X has chosen to reject me. This decision did not catch You by surprise. According to Your Word, all the days ordained for me were written in Your book before one of them came into existence (Psalm 139:16)—including the day X decided to reject me. It seems unfathomable that in Your Divine plan for my life, You, my loving Father, have allowed this situation to be. What is more amazing is that Your Word says You will cause it to work for my good (Romans 8:28).

Holy Spirit, thank You for shielding my heart from any permanent scarring from this trauma, this assault on my self-worth. Help me to accept X's rejection and not to get stuck wishing that he would have accepted me. Help me to understand that man's rejection is Your protection. Whatever You were protecting me from through X's rejection, I want to thank You. Thank You for my shield of faith that enables me to quench all the fiery darts of the enemy (Ephesians 6:16)—including this dart of rejection. It shall not pierce my soul.

Lord, thank You for the example Jesus set for me regarding how to respond to rejection from those close to me (Mark 6:4). I pray that You will give me that kind of immediate acceptance of the reality of rejection. I want the ability to keep moving forward with a positive attitude, and I realize that I can do it only by the power of Your Spirit (John 15:5).

I thank You, Father, for adopting me into Your family and

accepting me by the blood of my beloved Savior, Jesus Christ (Ephesians 1:6). I rejoice that I am Your child, Your heir and coheir with Christ (Romans 8:11). There is no higher honor, no greater level of acceptance in this life.

By Your grace, I choose to forgive this perpetrator of pain and to release him from any relational, emotional, or other obligation to me—including an apology. Turn X's heart toward You and cause him to stop rejecting Jesus and to embrace eternal salvation. In the name of Jesus, I pray. Amen.

Falsely Accused

Father, X has falsely accused me. I am appalled, hurt, and disappointed by this blatant lie. Notwithstanding, I am encouraged by the truth that no weapon formed against me will succeed because You will condemn every tongue that rises against me. Your vindicating me is my Divine benefit as Your servant (Isaiah 54:17). Father, only You can put this wicked person to shame and silence his lying lips for speaking against me (Psalm 31:17-18). I pray that You will cause his deceitful words to fall on deaf ears, to lose their impact, and find no fertile ground.

Help me not to fret about X's motive or that of others who choose to propagate this falsehood, for I know the real perpetrator is Satan, the father of lies (John 8:44), who goes around like a roaring lion looking for someone to devour (1 Peter 5:8). By Your grace, I will not be devoured by his scheme to bring discouragement, to derail me spiritually, or to destroy my peace. According to Your Word, I will count it all joy knowing that the testing of my faith produces patience (James 1:2-3).

I resist the temptation to retaliate. Father, give me the grace to respond like Jesus. When He was reviled, He did not revile in return; when He suffered, He did not threaten, but continued entrusting Himself to You who judge righteously (1 Peter 2:23). Help me to obey Your command to love my enemies, to bless those who curse me, to do good to those who hate me, and to pray for those who spitefully use me and persecute me with their lies (Matthew 5:44).

I can't do this in my own strength, but You, Father, work in me *to will* and *to do* of Your good pleasure (Philippians 2:13). I cast this care on You completely; I receive Your healing for my wounded emotions now.

As an act of obedience, I forgive X. I ask that You cause him to forsake his evil ways and submit to Christ as his Lord and Savior. In the name of Jesus, I pray. Amen.

Unjustly Fired

Father, my boss has unjustly fired me and I need Your help to respond with godly wisdom. Yes, I'm angry, but I know that You can calm my turbulent emotions. You are my refuge and my fortress (Psalm 91:2), my source of comfort and strength in facing the storms of life. Therefore, I cry out to You. I pour out my complaint before You. I declare before You my trouble. My spirit is overwhelmed within me; You know all aspects of this situation and the path that I should take (Palms 142:1-3).

Lord, should I just accept the boss's decision to fire me or should I protest it? Is my boss an agent in Your hands to push me out of my comfort zone and into my destiny, or is she an agent in Satan's plan to kill, steal, and destroy my livelihood? I stand still in Your presence now and wait patiently for You to act. I will not worry that the boss seems to be prospering in her way, neither will I fret about her wicked schemes. Yes, I will stop being angry, I will turn from my rage, and I will hold my temper for such responses only lead to harm (Psalm 37:7-8).

Father, I repent for viewing this job—even for a fleeting moment—as my source. Help me to remember that You supply all my needs according to Your riches in glory (Philippians 4:19). Help me to know that a job is simply a chosen channel of Your blessings for a chosen season and that as long as You are my Shepherd, I shall not lack (Psalm 23:1). So I say to my soul, "Wait silently for God alone, for my expectation is from Him" (Psalm 62:5).

I release forgiveness to my boss now. I pray You will bless her and give her wisdom, compassion, and discernment regarding all the members of her team. Thank You in advance for Your Divine plan to prosper me and to give me a future filled with hope (Jeremiah 29:11). Thank You for every person who will extend the favor I need to bring me into the next phase of my life. In the name of Jesus, I pray. Amen.

Betrayed by Spouse

Dear God, my husband and I vowed before You to be faithful to each other until death parted us. My husband has broken this covenant, betraying my trust and hurting me deeply. Although his decision to sin cannot be justified, I ask that You help me recognize and forsake any behavior on my part that may have contributed to his action.

Father, I realize that all have sinned and come short of Your glorious standards (Romans 3:23). Yes, I acknowledge that whenever I have sinned against You in any way, I committed spiritual adultery (James 4:4-5), and You have never wavered in Your forgiveness. Therefore, by the power of Your Spirit alone, I extend to my husband the same grace and mercy that You have extended to me.

Your Word declares that whomever You join together, no one should separate (Mark 10:9). I pray that the other woman, Satan's agent to try to destroy my marriage, will repent for her sin, for it is not Your will that anyone should be cut off from Your kingdom but that all should come to repentance (2 Peter 3:9).

I pray that You will restore and reignite the love between my husband and me for it's only through You that we can love unconditionally. With You all things are possible (Matthew 19:26). Fill my heart daily with compassion and patience toward my spouse. By Your grace, I put away all bitterness, wrath, and anger, along with all forms of malice (Colossians 3:8). Help me not to remind my husband of his failure or to attempt to retaliate in any way. I know that hanging on to my anger will only destroy me and put a barrier between You and me. Father, when the enemy floods my mind with thoughts of the betrayal, please help me to cast them down.

As we move forward, I ask that You lead us not into temptation but deliver us from every evil influence on our marriage (Matthew 6:13). I pray that we will trust in You with all our hearts and lean not to our understanding (Proverbs 3:5). As we walk in Your love, I believe You will renew and transform our relationship into a beautiful example of Your grace. In the name of Jesus, I pray. Amen.

Betrayed by Another

O Lord, I have become the victim of an untrustworthy friend, family member, coworker, or other. It is so hurtful and disappointing to know that someone I confided in has chosen to betray my trust and behave in a manner contrary to my best interests.

Lord, You knew beforehand that X was going to betray me. However, You neither warned me nor prevented it. Since You've allowed this trial to come into my life, I want to get the full value of the lesson I need to learn. I know it's going to work for my good in the end. One lesson I ask to learn immediately, dear Father, is to start listening more closely to the Holy Spirit, to get His guidance in deciding whom to trust with confidential information. I also ask for Your help in discerning if I am to salvage or sever my relationship with X.

Lord, only You know what seed of resentment, envy, insecurity, fear, greed, or other emotion lay at the root of this betrayal. Please reveal to X her true motive. Show her the error of her ways. Cause her to repent with great remorse and to make a lasting commitment to trust Jesus as her Lord and Savior.

Lord, I confess that I'm frustrated for putting myself in such a vulnerable position. How could I be so unaware, so undiscerning, or so trusting that I did not think to guard my heart? O Father, help me to believe that there are still some trustworthy people in all of my circles of interaction. Please help me not to isolate myself, to paint everybody with the same broad brush of mistrust, or go to any other relational extreme. Help me to move away from self-blame and remember that even Jesus became a victim of betrayal when Judas, one of His twelve disciples, told the enemy His whereabouts for thirty pieces of silver (Matthew 26:14-16).

So yes, Lord, I'll obey Your Word and extend forgiveness because if I do not forgive X for this trespass, You will not forgive my trespasses (Matthew 6:15). By Your grace, I will walk in love toward X and not succumb to bitterness or any form of retaliation. In the name of Jesus, I pray. Amen.

Financially Disadvantaged

Father, I have been financially disadvantaged in my dealings with X. By Your grace, I lay down my anger, frustration, disappointment, and unforgiveness. Because You guard all that is mine (Psalm 16:5), this outcome did not catch You by surprise. Help me put the loss in perspective and to remember that You can restore exceedingly and abundantly above all that I can ask or imagine (Ephesians 3:20).

Father, I need Your wisdom for how to proceed in resolving this matter—through legal channels or by simply forgiving the debt. I do not want to enable X to continue in her evil, dysfunctional, or irresponsible ways, but neither do I want to destroy her emotionally, financially, or otherwise. Show me where I may have failed to communicate or formally document my expectations. Help me to see if I set X up for failure with terms or conditions that were too vague, too onerous, or even too lenient.

O Lord, You know the current state of X's finances and whether she has the ability to repay me now or in the future. If she has dealt with me deceitfully, convict her of her sin. Your Word declares that bread gained by deceit is sweet, but afterward the deceiver's mouth will be full of gravel (Proverbs 20:17). I pray that X will find no satisfaction, profit, or peace in the fruit of her deception.

Give her the courage to come forward and resolve this issue in a manner that honors You. Let her not be named among the wicked who refuse to pay back what they owe (Psalm 37:21).

Rather, help her to become an upright person guided by integrity (Proverbs 11:3).

Father, thank You that You have made me a lender and not a borrower. I acknowledge that You own everything I possess (Psalm 24:1). I want to be a good, discerning steward of all You have entrusted into my care. Please do not let a root of bitterness spring up in me and stop me from helping others because of this disappointing outcome.

I submit this financial loss to You. I choose to walk in forgiveness and in the freedom-giving truth that You are the avenger of every wrong. In Jesus's name I pray. Amen.

Verbally Abused

Father God, You have said in Your Word that a crushed spirit is unbearable, worse than an illness (Proverbs 18:14). My spirit has been crushed by verbal abuse. "Death and life are in the power of the tongue" (Proverbs 18:21), and it feels as though part of me has been killed by someone else's words. Lord, the truth is that these words are lies from the heart of Satan, but I have heard them spoken so loudly, for so long, that they ring in my ears as though they were true. Father God, I renounce all the lies of the enemy spoken through the lips of people who should have been kind to me. These lies have told me I'm worthless, I'm guilty, I'm shameful, I will never amount to anything, and I do not deserve anything better. But Father, I receive Your Word and Your truth, and I come against the lies of verbal abuse.

I claim the reality of my new birth because in Christ, I am a child of the Most High God (John 1:12-13), an heir with Christ (Romans 8:17). I am seated with Christ at the right hand of God (Ephesians 2:6), I am cleansed from every sin (Hebrews 10:10), and I am the very righteousness of God in Christ, regardless of any mistakes I have made or will make (Romans 3:22-23). Father, I forgive this person who has verbally abused me, spoken ill of me, lied to me, and made me feel horrible. I put this person's sins against me under the cleansing blood of Jesus, and I receive the truth that Jesus paid for every sin.

Lord, fill me with Your Holy Spirit so that I will know what is true and what is false, and fill me with such confidence and peace in You that I will not be harmed by such words any longer. Father, touch this person's heart and heal it so that these desires to wound with words will die away in the light of Your love. Thank You, Father, for cleansing me of the pain of these lies and the burden of bitterness. In Jesus's name I pray. Amen.

Sexually Abused

Father, You are the God who sees me and hears me (Genesis 16:13), the one who is always with me even if my mother or father deserts me (Psalm 27:10). You are also the God who heals me. Now Father, I am in need of healing. You have seen the sexual abuse I have endured. You have heard my silent cries. You keep track of all my sorrows; You have collected all my tears in Your bottle (Psalm 56:8).

I was an innocent victim, undeserving of this abuse. I know that Jesus is touched by my pain, for He, though sinless, also suffered undeserved pain, humiliation, and even nakedness on the cross.

Father, this transgression against my body and my psyche is too much for me to carry alone. So I'm laying down the burden of betrayal, humiliation, shame, anger, grief, helplessness, and despair. I give the entire experience over to You. You are the God of all comfort (2 Corinthians 1:3-4). I trust in Your justice and Your mercy. Cause me not to replay the lies and threats that X spoke to diminish or intimidate me.

I renounce any emotional bondage or soul-tie that would try to keep my mind connected to this violator in any way. I ask that You take the sting out of the memories of this trying situation. Cleanse me from all traces of bitterness and renew within me Your peace and Your love.

Restore my confidence in the gifts and talents You have deposited in me. Help me to remember I am more than a conqueror through Jesus Christ who loves me (Romans 8:37). Thank You for restoring my innocence and my sexual purity. Only You can perform such a miracle.

Now, Lord, forgetting those things that are behind, I press toward the goals that are before me, the prize of Your high calling for my life (Philippians 3:13-14).

I claim X's soul for Your kingdom. I forgive him for everything he did to my body and my mind. I stand in the truth that my act of forgiveness disconnects me from the bondage of the past. Yes, Jesus has set me free and I am free indeed—free to enjoy healthy relationships and free to pursue my purpose. In the name of Jesus, I pray. Amen.

Physically Harmed

Father, X has harmed me physically, and my sense of fairness demands punishment. However, I know that I'm not better than my Savior, who experienced the ultimate physical aggression when He was crucified for my sins. His love for humankind caused Him to respond, "Father, forgive them, for they do not know what they do" (Luke 23:34). O Lord, help me to remember that the same Spirit resides in me and empowers me to respond in a similar manner. Yes, Lord, You work in me both to *will* and to *do* for Your good pleasure (Philippians 2:13). Therefore, by Your power alone, I cast down every revenge-filled thought regarding this situation. By faith, I declare that I am a mercy-filled child of God; thoughts of mercy permeate my mind and block every imagination that is displeasing to You. Thank You, Father, for giving me a merciful heart; it has positioned me to be blessed (Matthew 5:7).

Lord, even as I have chosen to release X for his violence against me, I pray that You will deliver him from whatever dysfunction he experienced in his painful history that causes him to inflict pain as a response to conflict. Teach him a better way to deal with life's adversities. Help him to understand that "all who draw the sword will die by the sword" (Matthew 26:52 NIV). I pray that X will become a person who is quick to hear, slow to speak, slow to anger (James 1:19). Most of all, I pray he will accept Jesus as his Lord and Savior.

Now Lord, I know that every adversity is an opportunity to

go to a higher place in You. I don't want to run from suffering or difficult situations. I want to be able to say like the psalmist that afflictions or troubles have been good for me as they've caused me to learn Your decrees (Psalm 119:71). Lord, I need special grace and agape love to look beyond X's faults and see his needs.

Clearly, he needs Jesus. Please do a work in my heart so that I have a burden for his soul and will be his self-appointed intercessor until You have wrought a mighty change in his life. In the name of Jesus, I pray. Amen.

Victim of Domestic Violence

Almighty God, You give power to the weak and strength to the powerless (Isaiah 40:29). I receive Your strength now to forgive X, who has subjected me to domestic violence. I pray You will help my children or others in my circle of influence to understand that by forgiving him, I am not condoning his actions or implying that his behavior is acceptable. I'm simply letting go of my desire to avenge the wrong he perpetrated against me.

Father, I pray that You will forgive me for tolerating X's abuse due to my various fears, my failure to trust You as my Provider and Protector, and my willingness to believe his vain promises to change.

Thank You for hearing my cry and opening the eyes of my understanding. I reject every lie the enemy told that kept me in bondage or that would lead me to put up with it in the future. I did not deserve the abuse; it was not my fault; I am not worthless. You have caused me to believe that I bring much value to the table in any relationship.

I forgive every well-meaning leader, advisor, or other person who misinterpreted Your Word and counseled me to submit to the abuse, believing it was Your will. O God, I pray that You will cause them to understand that Your command for wives to submit to their husbands also requires husbands to love their wives as their own bodies (Ephesians 5:28) and not to be harsh with them (Colossians 3:19).

I pray that You will arrest X's heart and cause him to say yes to salvation. Deliver him from his insecurities and the pain of his past. Heal him of his desire to control, manipulate, and abuse a woman he claims to love. I release him now, by the power of Your Spirit. I put away all bitterness and thoughts of wrath (Ephesians 4:31-32). I pray that You will help me to be an ambassador of wisdom as I encourage other women caught in the web of domestic violence to trust You and to find safety. In the name of Jesus, I pray. Amen.

Loved One Harmed

Father, X has inflicted harm or violence against someone I love dearly. I know that my desire to see him experience the same or greater pain is a result of my carnal thinking. I need Your help now. Your Word says that if I walk in the Spirit—letting Him guide my life—I will not give in to my sinful nature. Lord, You know my sinful nature wants to do evil, which is just the opposite of what the Spirit wants (Galatians 5:16-26). I call upon You, Holy Spirit, to let love and self-control (Galatians 5:23) prevail right now.

Lord, by Your grace I release X from this trespass against my loved one. My forgiveness is not dependent on justice being served, his showing remorse, or his offering an apology—none of which may ever happen. I simply release him as an act of my will in obedience to Your Word. Therefore, I lay this offense at Your feet. I want to pass this spiritual test, O Lord. You test the righteous, but You hate the wicked and the one who loves violence (Psalm 11:5). You said vengeance and payback belong to You (Deuteronomy 32:35).

Beyond Your justice, which is far above earthly justice, I ask You to do a work in X's heart and mind and deliver him from his violent ways. Jesus said that whatever we bind on earth will be bound in heaven (Matthew 18:18). Therefore, I bind the spirit of violence and pray that X will cease to operate under its influence. Cause him to repent of his sin and to submit to the lordship of Jesus Christ.

I pray that X's aggression will not scar my loved one emotionally. Father, You sent Your Son to bind up the brokenhearted (Isaiah 61:1) and to dry every tear (Revelation 21:4). I trust You to comfort and heal the heart of my loved one, for Your love for him is even greater than mine. In the name of Jesus, I pray. Amen.

Humiliated

Father, X has humiliated me and caused me to feel "less than" Your Word says I am in Your sight. Each time I replay the scene and relive that diminishing moment, my anger is rekindled. X's insensitive words almost caused me to forget who I am in You, but Your truth prevailed: You decided in advance to adopt me into Your own family by bringing me to Yourself through Jesus Christ. This is what You wanted to do, and it gave You great pleasure (Ephesians 1:5). Therefore, I denounce the voice of the enemy speaking through X's words and actions.

Without regard to my feelings and in obedience to Your Word, I choose to forgive X for her degrading words and actions. I ask You to bless her, Lord, with an outpouring of Your love and the deep knowledge of Your grace. Deal with her regarding any malice or jealousy in her heart. Cleanse her from all unrighteousness. Cause her to become a woman who opens her mouth with wisdom, whose tongue operates under the law of kindness (Proverbs 31:26), and who builds others up rather than tearing them down.

Lord, You desire me to be truthful in my innermost being (Psalm 51:6); therefore, I admit that a large part of my anger is attributable to my pride, my desire to project a certain image. X's words cut me to my core; I felt I lost stature and dignity in the eyes of those present. I realize this reveals my dependence on others to validate my self-worth. O Lord, deliver me from such bondage thinking and give me the desire to seek Your approval only and not to be a pleaser of people (Colossians 3:22). Help me to remember that my Savior suffered the ultimate humiliation by dying on a cross for my sins, despising the shame of it all (Hebrews 12:2).

Lord, I surrender my anger to You. Please remove any bitterness toward X from my heart so that I can grow closer to You and be more conformed to the image of Your Son (Romans 8:29). In the name of Jesus, I pray. Amen.

Discriminated Against

Father, X has discriminated against me. I need Your direction whether to ignore it or to protest it through proper channels. Help me to remember that despite someone preferring another over me in a prejudicial way, no one can thwart Your plan and purpose for my life (Isaiah 14:27).

I proclaim the words of the psalmist, "All the days *ordained* for me were written in your book before one of them came to be" (Psalm 139:16 NIV). Yes, Father, You have ordained my destiny. Therefore, I resist all anxiety about other people's judgment of me based on my gender, race, height, weight, economic or social status, or any other aspect of my being. We are all one in Your eyes whether Jew or Gentile, slave or free, male or female (Galatians 3:28). You see not as people see; for people look at outward appearance, but You look at the heart (1 Samuel 16:7).

By Your grace, I will not be frustrated by any show of partiality. Rather, I will focus on maintaining a righteous attitude and staying in right standing with You; then You will surround me with favor like a shield (Psalm 5:12). Father, You can turn hearts toward me that never intended to show me favor. Even the heart of a king or others in places of authority are in Your hand, and You have the power to turn their minds in any direction You please (Proverbs 21:1). Grant me favor, O Lord, with my bosses, customers, and the critical players within my circle of interaction.

I pray for every person or institution that condones

discriminatory practices. I ask that You open the eyes of their understanding so they will know that You do not show partiality but You accept every man and woman who fears You and does what is right (Acts 10:34-35). Let me be quick to forgive the perpetrators of discrimination. Let my reactions be acceptable in Your sight.

Help me not to lean on my own understanding and get frustrated when it seems that discrimination is succeeding. Rather, let my faith arise and let me stand on Your promises with my joy intact for the entire world to see. In the name of Jesus, I pray. Amen.

Wrongly Incarcerated

O Lord, You know that I'm innocent of the crime I'm serving time for. I need You to restore my faith in the justice system and help me to resist the root of bitterness that is trying to take hold of my heart. In obedience to Your command to forgive, and enabled by Your grace, I release every corrupt witness, unfair judge, biased or manipulated juror, and inept attorney who caused me to be incarcerated. They opened their mouths against me. You saw them. However, You have not left me alone. Your Word declares that You hear the groaning of the prisoner (Psalm 102:20) and You do not let a false witness go unpunished (Proverbs 19:9).

O Lord; be not silent! Be not far from me! Awake and rouse Yourself for my vindication, for my cause, my God and my Lord (Psalm 35:21-23). You know the truth of my situation for there is nothing hidden from You. Reveal it, O Lord. I cry out to You as my only hope. Let justice roll down like waters, and righteousness like an ever-flowing stream (Amos 5:24).

I declare that You have strategically placed somebody with the right influence to plead my cause, to help me secure my freedom. I take courage from the testimony of Joseph the Old Testament Jewish patriarch sold into slavery, falsely accused of raping his master's wife, and thrown into prison as a consequence. Oh God, You orchestrated his phenomenal release overnight and promoted him to the position of right-hand man to the king of Egypt (Genesis 37–50). Lord, I believe that as You delivered him so miraculously, You can show Yourself strong in my situation. My eyes are on You to meet all my needs according to Your great resources in heaven (Philippians 4:19).

Lord, let me not become weary as I wait for Your intervention. Cause me to redeem the time by sharing Your love and truth with fellow prisoners as well as the guards. Let my joy and passion for You bring many souls into Your kingdom. By Your grace, I will walk in the spiritual and emotional freedom that comes from forgiveness while I wait for my release at the appointed time. In the name of Jesus, I pray. Amen.

Misunderstood

Father, I need to forgive those who have misunderstood my actions. I am angered and frustrated by this because I believe that my deeds sprang from a pure heart with right intentions. Notwithstanding, because You desire me to be truthful in my innermost being (Psalm 51:6), I ask You to search me now and know my heart; test me and reveal any hidden motives. Point out anything in me that offends You and others, and lead me along the path of everlasting life (Psalm 139:23-24).

I pray that You will show me how I may have contributed to this misunderstanding through poor or unwise communication, a proud attitude, or any other blind spot. Teach me how to be an effective communicator who respects everybody's right to have an opinion that differs from mine. Cause me and my accusers to forsake any unrighteous agenda or ulterior motives and to desire Your perfect will in this situation.

I pray Your blessings upon those who have misunderstood me. Give them the courage to communicate their concerns to me directly in a way that honors You so that ultimately they too will experience Your peace. Help me to listen and to be receptive to whatever message You want me to receive from them.

I know that it is not Your will for me to be anxious about anything (Philippians 4:6). Therefore, I release all anxiety about the outcome of this matter; I cast all my cares concerning it upon You (1 Peter 5:7). I rejoice in knowing that, as my heavenly

Father, You are able to do exceedingly, abundantly above all that I can ask or think in resolving this matter (Ephesians 3:20).

Therefore, by the power of Your Holy Spirit, I forgive every person who has spoken a negative word against me and I forsake all thoughts of any form of retaliation. I stand on the promise that no weapon formed against me will succeed. You will silence every voice that rises up to accuse me, for Your vindication is a benefit that I enjoy as Your servant (Isaiah 54:17). In the name of Jesus, I pray. Amen.

Manipulated

Father, it's clear that X has manipulated me for his personal gain. I am extremely angry with him, but also very angry and disappointed with myself for not discerning his motives. Please help me to forgive myself for being ignorant of Satan's tactics (2 Corinthians 2:11). Had I acknowledged You in all my ways, You would have directed my path (Proverbs 3:5) and caused me to avoid this situation altogether. I'm so sorry. Please forgive me. By Your grace, I will make every effort to forsake my independent ways, for I know that apart from You, I can do nothing (John 15:5).

Father, this manipulation has hurt me deeply. Anger and feelings of betrayal constantly occupy my mind. Satan bombards me with thoughts of retaliation all day long. Help me to close my ears to him and to open my heart to trust You to avenge this wrong, for You have warned, "It is mine to avenge; I will repay" (Deuteronomy 32:35 NIV). By faith, I release my anger, indignation, and frustration into Your hands. I cast down every evil imagination and scenario of revenge and bring every thought into subjection to the Holy Spirit (2 Corinthians 10:5).

As an act of my will, I choose to forgive X because You forgive my transgressions. Cleanse me now from all bitterness and renew a right spirit within me (Psalm 51:10) so that my light may shine even brighter in this dark world. I pray You will deal with X and cause him to see the error of his ways. I pray that he will accept Jesus as his Savior. Fill him with Your love and compassion and drive out covetousness, disregard for other's wishes, and all unrighteousness.

Finally, Father, I ask You to refill me with Your Holy Spirit and give me discernment so that I will be wise as a serpent but harmless as a dove (Matthew 10:16). Thank You for Your healing grace and for guiding my steps back to You when I miss the mark. In the name of Jesus, I pray. Amen.

Passed Over

Lord, I have been passed over for the promotion I had my heart set on. I am disappointed, and yes, even humiliated by this decision because I believe I am the best person for the position. Enabled by Your Spirit, I forgive every person who was involved in the decision. I forgive them for any preferential treatment or biases that came into play in their deciding to give the post to another.

I put away anger and resentment. I pray You will bless the person who was selected for this assignment. Cause me to work in harmony with him, for unity is the place where You command a blessing (Psalm 133:1,3).

I find comfort in Your Word that assures me that promotion doesn't come from the east, nor from the west, nor from the south, but You are the judge. You put down one and exalt another (Psalm 75:6). You rule in the affairs of men and give positions to whomever You please (Daniel 4:17). I know that You have plans to prosper me, to give me a future filled with hope (Jeremiah 29:11). I call upon Your Holy Spirit to help me move forward with hope, determination, and a positive attitude. Please do not let me sabotage my future by a wrong response to this disappointment. Help me to remember that had it been Your Divine plan to grant me this promotion, no one could have stopped it. When You stretch forth Your hand and purpose a thing, no one can thwart it (Isaiah 14:27).

You bless and surround with favor those who are in right

standing with You (Psalm 5:12). I want to always be in right standing with You, O Lord, and to submit to those in authority over me with all grace. Search me and shine the light on any pride in my heart causing me to think more highly of myself than I ought (Romans 12:3). Further, show me the areas where I need to sharpen my skills technically, relationally, or socially.

As I continue in my current position, let excellence be my norm. Help me to remember that whatever I do, I must do it as if I'm doing it for You and not for people (Colossians 3:17).

In Jesus's name I pray. Amen.

Offended

Father, I am offended and hurt by X's behavior toward me. I realize that each time I rehearse the situation, it prevents me from experiencing Your peace. I know that in this life, offenses will come—intentionally or unintentionally. Help me to remember that all things work together for my good because I love You and I am called according to Your purpose (Romans 8:28). You could have prevented this offense, but You have allowed it to come into my life for a specific purpose. Please do not let me miss the spiritual growth, the improved relational skills, or any other benefit that will result from my handling this situation Your way.

Your Word says that those who are merciful are blessed and will obtain mercy (Matthew 5:7). Father, give me a merciful heart toward X. Help me to extend to him the same mercy that You so faithfully extend to me when I violate Your commands.

Proverbs 19:11 reminds me that wisdom gives me patience and that it is to my glory to overlook an offense. Father, I do not want to get stuck in this offense for it is just a trap of the evil one to set me back spiritually and emotionally.

Give me the wisdom to determine when to overlook an offense versus when to confront it. If a godly confrontation is indeed Your will in this situation, then give me the courage to go privately to X and tell him his fault (Matthew 18:15). I pray that I will use the right words—Your words—to express my true feelings and bring reconciliation and harmony. I know that

Your words, spoken through me, will not fall to the ground, but will succeed in accomplishing Your purpose (Isaiah 55:11).

Father, as much as it depends on me and as Your grace prevails, I will make every effort to live peaceably with everybody (Romans 12:18). Therefore, by the power of the Holy Spirit, I let go of this offense now. In the name of Jesus, I pray. Amen.

Taken for Granted

Lord, I am feeling resentful toward X because I serve her faithfully and she takes my efforts for granted. I need to forgive her for her attitude of entitlement, for not expressing gratitude, and for not demonstrating concern for my needs or personal well-being. I know that becoming resentful is contrary to Your desire for me to be a cheerful giver of my time, talent, and resources (2 Corinthians 9:7).

Help me to acknowledge and resist the fears, insecurities, false guilt, or even the manipulation that cause me to tolerate X's ingratitude. Help me to develop and clearly communicate new boundaries and preferences to govern my interactions with her so that her needs and expectations are not the driving force in our relationship.

I acknowledge responsibility for helping to create this situation, and even for seeking my own gratification in the form of accolades, acceptance, or fulfillment of my need to be needed. I realize when I serve with ulterior motives, I am bound to encounter selfish people who take me for granted. Help me, Lord. Show me if I need to reduce, restructure, or even eliminate my service to her. I need a wise solution to this problem; I don't want to go from one extreme to another in my service.

I want to obey Your admonition to work wholeheartedly at whatever I do, as though I work for You rather than for people. I want to always remember that You will give me an inheritance as Your reward, and that the one I am serving is Christ (Colossians 3:23-24).

Lord, I desire to maximize the gifts You have given me to serve others, and I want to do it joyfully. Therefore, if my gift is to encourage others, I want to be encouraging. If it is giving, help me to give generously. If You have given me leadership ability, help me take the responsibility seriously. And if I have a gift for showing kindness to others, let me do it gladly. I don't want to just pretend to love others; I want to really love them (Romans 12:8-10).

By faith and with hope in Your resolution of this situation, I release my resentment and go forward in the strength of the Holy Spirit.

General Forgiveness Prayer[12]

Father, X has perpetrated a wrong against me. You require me to forgive her or You will not forgive my sins (Matthew 6:15). You saw this transgression long before it happened, and in Your infinite wisdom You allowed it to occur anyway. Therefore, I know that You will cause it to work for my good because I love You and I am called according to Your purpose (Romans 8:28).

I ask You to heal my emotional pain from this hurt and to keep it from scarring my heart. I give up my desire to avenge this wrong because You said that vengeance belongs to You and that You will repay those who deserve it (Deuteronomy 32:35). Enabled by Your grace, I put away all bitterness, wrath, anger, and evil speaking (Ephesians 4:31-32). I place my full faith in You, O Lord, to judge righteously and to avenge this wrong. Notwithstanding, I extend mercy to my perpetrator, knowing that I'm planting seeds to reap mercy when I will need it.

Help me to understand that while forgiveness is mandatory, reconciliation with the offender is not always required. Therefore, I need Your wisdom to discern whether to restore, redefine, or release this relationship. Grant me the courage and the grace to respond according to Your perfect will.

As an act of my will and in obedience to Your command to forgive if I wish to be forgiven, I release X from this offense and free her of all obligation—even that of offering me an apology. Your Word says that if X sins against me as often as seventy times seven, that I must forgive her (Matthew 18:21-22). Now, Father,

You know that I could not possibly do this in my own strength; I need Your Divine empowerment.

I thank You for the lesson that I will learn from this situation and the growth I will experience as I grant forgiveness now. In the name of Jesus, I pray. Amen.

Notes

1. Christopher Dorner's Manifesto, http://ktla.com/2013/02/12/read-christopher -dorners-so-called-manifesto/.

2. This story was retold to me by my friend Diane Gardner. For the complete account of family deception, unforgiveness, and heartbreak, please read her groundbreaking memoir, *Overcoming the Enemy's Storms* (Bloomington, IN: WestBow Press, 2014).

3. Gardner, *Overcoming the Enemy's Storms*, 276.

4. Kevin M. Carlsmith, Timothy D. Wilson, Daniel T. Gilbert, "The Paradoxical Consequences of Revenge," *Journal of Personality and Social Psychology*, vol. 95, December 2008, 1316-24.

5. Bob and Audrey Meisner, *Marriage Undercover: Thriving in a Culture of Quiet Desperation* (Orrstown, PA: MileStones International Publishers, 2004), Kindle edition, location 699-703, 806-8.

6. Christian Broadcasting Network, *700 Club*, "Bob and Audrey Meisner: A Wife's Betrayal," www.cbn.com/tv/1521757736001 (accessed December 14, 2014).

7. Meisner, *Marriage Undercover*, location 958-68.

8. Christian Broadcasting Network, *700 Club*, "A Wife's Betrayal."

9. Adam Hamilton, *Forgiveness: Finding Peace Through Letting Go* (Nashville, TN: Abingdon Press, 2012), Kindle edition, location 50-55.

10. Fred Luskin, *Forgive for Good: A Proven Prescription for Health and Happiness* (San Francisco: Harper San Francisco, 2002), 77-93.

11. Jim Dincalci, *How to Forgive When You Can't: The Breakthrough Guide to Free Your Heart and Mind* (Tallahassee, FL: Ruah Press, 2011), Kindle edition, location 1556-57.

12. Adapted from Deborah Smith Pegues, *Emergency Prayers* (Eugene, OR: Harvest House Publishers, 2008), 73.

About the Author

Deborah Smith Pegues is an international speaker, award-winning author, a Bible teacher, certified public accountant, and certified behavioral consultant specializing in understanding personality temperaments. She and her husband, Darnell, have been married for over 36 years and live in California.

For speaking engagements, please contact her at:
The Pegues Group
P.O. Box 56382
Los Angeles, CA 90056
(323) 293-5861
Email: deborah@confrontingissues.com
www.confrontingissues.com

Other books by Deborah Smith Pegues:

- *30 Days to Taming Your Tongue*
  (nearly one million copies sold)
- *Emergency Prayers*
- *Choose Your Attitude, Change Your Life*
- *30 Days to Taming Your Finances*
- *Confronting Without Offending*
- *Socially Smart in 60 Seconds*
- *30 Days to a Stronger, More Confident You*

30 Days to
Taming Your Tongue

What You Say (and Don't Say)
Will Improve Your Relationships

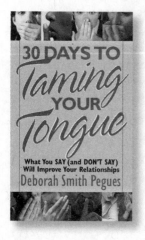

Certified behavioral consultant Deborah Pegues knows how easily a slip of the tongue can cause problems in personal and business relationships. This is why she wrote the popular *30 Days to Taming Your Tongue*. Her 30-day devotional will help you not only tame your tongue but make it productive rather than destructive.

With humor and a bit of refreshing sass, Deborah devotes chapters to learning how to overcome the

- retaliating tongue
- know-it-all tongue
- belittling tongue
- hasty tongue
- gossiping tongue
- 25 more!

Short stories, anecdotes, soul-searching questions, and scripturally based personal affirmations combine to make each chapter applicable and life changing.

Choose Your Attitude, Change Your Life ...in 30 Days

You've heard the expression, "Attitude is everything." But can a positive mental attitude make all that much difference in your personal and professional life? Deborah Smith Pegues, author of the bestselling *30 Days to Taming Your Tongue*, believes strongly that it can.

In *Choose Your Attitude, Change Your Life*, Deborah explores the root causes of 30 negative attitudes, their impact on your life and relationships, and how you can learn to think positively instead. As a result, she helps you recognize and conquer counterproductive behaviors, such as criticizing the choices others make, being inflexible, and being indifferent to the needs of others.

Deborah's handy guide uses Bible-based principles and practical strategies to point you toward the path to a better outlook on life, empowering you to display a positive mental attitude in every situation and leading to healthier relationships, personal growth, and the ability to handle life's challenges as never before.

Previously titled *30 Days to a Great Attitude*.

Is insecurity robbing you of life's fullness?

You can understand and overcome the fears that limit you. And you can build the confidence you need to reach your personal and professional goals.

30 Days to a Stronger, More Confident You uses biblical and present-day examples to help you discover the secrets to bold and fearless living at home, at work, and at play. Strategies such as resting in God's Word, resisting intimidation, and remembering past victories provide an effective plan of attack on self-doubt. You'll also learn how to

- value individuality
- establish boundaries
- conquer perfectionism
- empower others
- embrace success

Through Scripture-based principles, heart-searching personal challenges, and healing prayers and affirmations, you will discover the path to a more successful you.

30 Days to Taming Your Kid's Tongue

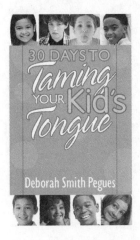

Learning to control the tongue is a lifelong pursuit. That's why it's so important for you as parents to help your children learn to tame their tongues from the moment they begin to talk.

Certified behavioral consultant Deborah Pegues offers invaluable insights for parents who long to help their children learn not only what to say and how to say it, but also what *not* to say. With humor and wisdom, Deborah devotes chapters to teaching your kids such important lessons as

- speaking respectfully to an adult
- using their indoor voice
- knowing when to speak up and when to remain quiet
- giving and accepting compliments
- expressing anger appropriately
- admitting mistakes or wrongdoing
- talking to God

Stories, soul-searching questions, and scripturally based personal affirmations combine to make each reading applicable and life changing for you and your family.

To learn more about Harvest House books and
to read sample chapters, visit our website:

www.harvesthousepublishers.com

HARVEST HOUSE PUBLISHERS
EUGENE, OREGON